Walking This Walk

How Hard Places Determine Who We Are And What We Believe

by
Brad Erlandson

Table of Contents

Dedication

I would like to dedicate the book to any who have suffered in any way and have had their suffering compounded by those who, like Job's comforters, may have wanted to help, but essentially brought more pain to an already hard situation. May you find God's comfort.

Acknowledgments

There are so many people I would like to thank and to mention. I know there are some I may forget as I write this, but I want to make an attempt to thank all those who I can remember.

First, I would like to thank Dan Macalliff. He led my sister, Gretchen, to Christ and in turn was instrumental in my conversion; without his faith and obedience, I would not be here. I would like to thank Dr. Koshey and Dwight Craver who established the "Discipleship House" on the Syracuse University Campus. Their faith and teaching established my faith. To all the professors at Toccoa Falls Bible College who taught and tested me, especially Dr. Collier and Dr. Easly, thank you for your steadfast faith.

Thank you to my friends Jeff Tatarsky and Chris Todd, who helped me so greatly when I was struggling with issues at college and in establishing the church. They are pillars in the faith. To "Holy" Hubert Lindsey who, by his example, challenged me greatly to be a strong and bold voice for God. To Loren Covarrubius, who balanced out some things that were out of balance in my thinking and prophesied a strong word over my wife and me. He was instrumental in bringing much healing into my wife's and my life. To all my friends at Oakland Christian Church who were there when I needed them the most. They encouraged me when I was down and spoke words of life to me. For all the authors of books that I've read that encouraged me, I would like to thank my friend Dr. Peter Keelin, Attorney at Law, John Leh and my dentist, Mark Stabley for all your help and support. Thanks to all my therapists and trainers who have helped me get better physically. (John Piper, Watchman Nee, A.W. Tozer, Oswald Chambers and many others).

For the early church fathers who stood up for the Truth and became a great "cloud of witnesses" and example.

For my mom and dad and my sisters, Lindy and Gretchen, for putting up with me in the early years.

For my wife, Suzanne, and two sons, Bradley and Paul; without your support, I would not be here.

I salute you one and all and may the Lord be with you all forever more.

Foreword

I have written this brief memoir of my life in order to possibly aid someone in their relationship with God. It is my hope to help them better understand how the unpredictability of life and the movements of our thinking, both natural and theological, can help us to develop a closer walk with God and to more fully grasp our purpose for being on this planet.

I'm aware that most people do not have large amounts of time to read the Bible or any other theological book that may help them to find God and His purpose in a clearer way. There are many excellent theological works that you can read and that I would urge you to read; I could have written such a book but have refrained. There are many great books, but the problem is that with reading, we only experience the thing that we are reading at one level. All of what we read in the Bible, for example, is true, but if we don't apply it to our lives, it is like looking at a cool pool of water on a hot day, imagining how it would be jumping in, but not jumping in and experiencing the cool water on our body. We don't enter in to the fullness of the experience because we haven't jumped in.

At the same time we have to know how to apply what we read. Not all that we read in the Bible is to be applied directly in the sense that we must "do" something, but rather it is for our understanding's sake. When understanding comes to us, it edifies us and causes us to see things the way they are in a clearer way. But regardless, when we read, we only experience what we are reading on one level. Reading is a blessing and is a gift from God but by its nature can only take us so far.

If you read a story about a great hero who rescued many people from certain danger it may inspire you to be more heroic, but in reality that was not you rescuing the people, it was someone else. You read about the hero and you experienced that event in your mind, but to actually do what he did is an experience on a whole different level. In his epistle to the Ephesians (3:1-7), the apostle Paul talks about the revelation that he received, saying, "when you read you may understand my knowledge in the mystery of Christ." Paul received it and then transmitted it to us. Similarly, the prophet Isaiah "saw the Lord" (Isaiah 6:1), and he wrote down what he saw. We neither had the revelation that Paul had nor have we seen God like Isaiah did, but when we read, somehow with the help of the Spirit, we can see it on one level.

In April, 2002, I was struck by a drunk driver and paralyzed from the waist down. When I taught apologetics (the defense of the Christian faith), we would talk about the issue of suffering. What I believe the

Bible is saying is that God is good and suffering is real. The question, if God is all love, then why all the suffering because absolute love would stop it and absolute power could stop it. This argument has been used by atheists and agnostics throughout history in order to find fault with God and support their life-styles which, in many cases, were self-centered.

In other words, with this logic, God is not real, and if He is not real, then anything goes in terms of behavior. It seems logical but it misses the ultimate point: what is the purpose of life? Is the purpose of this life that we would live here on Earth with no prob-lems or sufferings? If that is true, then the first ques-tion makes complete sense. However, if it is not true, if God's will incorporates suffering into His plan and it has an ultimate purpose, then the first question is the wrong question. With that said, I taught suffering from the purely mental and Biblical perspective; but now I experience it on a whole new level.

A main point I want to make in this book is that just because you are suffering on one level or another, that does not mean that you are somehow singled out for God's punishment. What you are going through is by divine design and has a real purpose. You must accept this. Some teach that as a Christian you will avoid all suffering and live healthy and wealthy all your days. Those who embrace this teaching often lose faith when hard times come.

Many of God's people in the Bible and throughout history have struggled and suffered. It has been in these hard times that God came to them in a special way. Being in hard places forces us to determine what we really believe and who we really are. A relationship with God cannot be forced but it can be urged.

That has been my goal in this effort. I have had the opportunity to spend five years at a Bible college and an additional three years earning a Master's Degree in Religion. I have been in ministry situations all my Christian life. I have been involved in evangelism as an associate and youth pastor. I have experienced non-denominational as well as denominational activity–good and bad–as a member of both.

In studying the Bible for a long time, I have noticed that God says a lot in a few words. The Bible is comprised of sixty-six books, and God used forty different authors over a period of four thousand years, saying many things but with relatively few words. Jesus told stories to communicate His message. The four Gospels are not long, but are packed with great amounts of information. They contain the life and teachings of Jesus–not all the history of Jesus, but all we need to grasp who He is, what He did, and how it relates to us as people, now and throughout history.

So, this story will not be long but my hope is that it will help the reader to see a person in modern times wrestling with a relationship with God and grappling with His purpose. I use my life as a story realizing that when people read a story they not only tend to stay interested they also are better able to grasp the truths though the story. God's word is really "His-Story."

We all love a good story.

Chapter One

Early Life in the Sixties and Seventies

I was born in Seneca Falls, New York, on June 10, 1958. When I was four years-old, we moved to Camillus, N.Y., about twenty minutes west of Syracuse. My parents raised my two sisters and me as Episcopalian. My Dad was a Methodist, but I guess he conceded to my Mom in the area of the spiritual upbringing of the children. The truth is, that though my parents attended church and were aware of the spiritual dimension, I was oblivious to anything that related to God or His Word. The Bible was not read in our home, and I think that there was a general disagreement between my parents that, over time, became a problem for my two sisters and me.

You don't see the difference when you're a little kid, but when you get older and look back on the whole situation it becomes clearer. My dad, for example, on Sundays, instead of going to church, would take me to hockey when I was younger, and to work when I got older, giving me the impression that church and God were not that important. At the time, I did not really think about it, and my mother never said anything about it that I can recall. My dad never told me about God or tried to persuade me to believe. I truly loved my dad and hold nothing against him, but in my family spiritual things were not a priority because my dad did not guard, guide and govern the family in a Biblical sense. He provided well for us and showed us great love but he did not "pass the blessing" of understanding the God of the Bible.

I grew up in a middle class suburb. My dad was a salesman, and my mom was a "stay-at home-mom," and raised myself and my two sisters. When I was about ten years-old, she decided to go to work. I'm not sure if she went out of necessity or because my dad wanted her to, or if she just wanted to. To this day, I still don't know the real reason.

In the late Sixties, things in America were changing. Much of the culture was shifting away from basic common-sense living that was really grounded in a clear sense of right and wrong, a belief in the Bible and absolute truth, to an "everything-is-relative" mind set. The concept of "absolutes" was no longer being taught, and now everything was up for grabs in terms of thinking. The rock music captured the thinking of much of the youth of the nation. The music and the lyrics were permeating the culture. Much of the content was focused on man and all that he could do for himself to make his life better, whether it was morally right or not. Lyric refrains like "take the money and run" or "tonight's the night, it's going to be alright"set the cultural tone, the main focus being on self-gratification, no matter who is affected.

Many say song lyrics are just words, and they don't have any effect. But words have meaning, and if you're not taught absolutes, then you have no container to put what you're hearing in. You have nothing to compare it to. Many even today think if it's on TV or radio, then it must be alright.

I remember when the Woodstock concert happened; it seemed like a big deal, and it *was* a big deal for older people. But at the time, I was around nine years old and, for me, it had little meaning. I did not realize at the time the culture was shifting dramatically. The hippies were coming and the Haight-Ashbury winds were blowing west from California (Haight and Ashbury were two intersecting streets in San Francisco, which became a well-known neighborhood where hippies from all over the nation congregated). In1965-67, young people were trying to find purpose in sex, drugs and rock and roll. It came to be called the "summer of love," and the youth were looking for new consciousness and enlightenment. Timothy Leary, a former-Harvard-professor-turned-LSD-guru, was telling people to "turn on, tune in and drop out."

I was still very young when the concepts of the rock scene filtered their way into the culture. This was not your Frank Sinatra or Buddy Holly, the relatively innocent music of the Forties and Fifties. Their relatively tame music was being replaced by the rush of the Beatles, Jimi Hendrix, the Rolling Stones and the like. "Imagine there's no heaven," sang John Lennon of the Beatles. This music became popular and, though some of it was relatively innocent, it seemed to open a door to a philosophy that pushed the idea of God, Jesus and absolute truth away from the mainstream of the American mind set.

And that was just the beginning. The Beatles opened the way for the many other bands of the Sixties and Seventies to arise. No doubt many were talented and were not totally anti-God, but the majority were preaching a message of, "if it feels good do it," and young people began to abuse drugs and alcohol on a massive scale. I think that the parents of that generation were really taken by surprise. Though the parents would participate in the drinking parties of their own, the thought of illegal drugs never entered their minds.

I remember James Dobson, the founder of the "Focus on the Family" radio ministry saying that he once asked his dad (who was a preacher before the sixties) if he ever worried about him getting into those kinds of things (drugs, sexual immorality and rebellion). His father said, never, it didn't even enter his mind, at all. Man, the good old days. I have teenagers now and this culture screams at them all the time to do whatever they want. The younger generation of the late Sixties and early Seventies was saying to the older generation, "Hey you do your drinking, we have marijuana, LSD and other drugs. This is *our* generation."

I have to say that I have learned a great deal from my parents, both good and bad. I have also looked back at the culture of the Sixties and Seventies and have determined that much of what was going on contributed to my personal rebellion. I am not saying that I had no responsibility; obviously, we are all accountable for our actions. I can say with no question, however, that my behavior was encouraged by the lack of parental discipline (like many parents back then my folks were great with the love part, but weak with the discipline part) and a culture that no longer accepted the idea that things were right and wrong simply because God said so. When I look back, these two things were instrumental parts of my rebellious attitude.

No parent teaches or wants their kids to rebel and do wrong. Some kids are like wild stallions that need a strong hand. Not all parents are equipped emotionally or spiritually to tame these wild ones, and consequently the children run wild until they run into reality. That was me. The culture that was saying "anything goes," and my parents were not ready for this onslaught. Every general knows that the surprise attack is best; the enemy "came in like a flood" for sure and took that generation by surprise.

Today the same Devil prowls about like a roaring lion and is seeking to destroy young people. Some of the same things are in place (sex, drugs, etc.) but other influences have come in as well. The new media, including video games, cable TV and the Internet, have made it easy for young men to become obsessed at an early age with pornography and rebellion against parents. "Virtual reality" has turned many into zombies that want little to do with the responsibilities of real life and have very little social skills. Because it is so easy to become mentally detached through obsession with the Internet, video games and TV, the tendency is to have little ambition to want to be involved in real life.

My first fifteen years were pretty typical of the average middle class American lifestyle full of friends, organized sports and family vacations. I played a lot of sports, including hockey, lacrosse, baseball, soccer, football, running and weightlifting. I had my share of victories and defeats in all the sports I competed in. I played on two bantam-level teams (thirteen and fourteen year-olds) in youth hockey one season. On one I was captain of the team, and the other team I was on won the league championship. I made the high school hockey team my freshman year and played all four years. My love for hockey has been long-lasting, and into adulthood, I coached youth hockey and played in a men's league.

Early on, though, I did try other sports. I was cut from the seventh-grade football team, but made the eighth-grade team. In football, I played quarterback and cornerback. I was becoming fairly good at both, and I kick myself to this day that I did not continue to play football. When I was in ninth grade, I decided to play soccer, for some reason. That was my last year of soccer or football, I never played after that. I think my size had something to do with it, but I also think that other factors were beginning to play into it.

Acceptance is huge when you're fifteen years-old, and if you're not exceptional as an athlete or you lack size, you are no longer accepted by those who are big and talented. I felt at the time that I was being overlooked by coaches and only the "suck-ups" were getting playing time. This was partially right and partially wrong. My size and skill were an issue, but I wish that some coach would have encouraged me to try harder or give me some direction, but it never happened. Regretfully many coaches have only one objective, which is to win at all cost. As a result, many decent players who would have played and done well over time fall through the cracks and then look for acceptance in other ways. Which, for me, was the way of acceptance through the party life style.

In the late Sixties and early Seventies, the Vietnam War was creating a rift in the American mind set. The war was causing many to begin to protest, as they believed that the war was wrong. Many violently shook their fist at the government as many of our men were being killed in battle. Students on college campuses held protests and "peace" rallies. Some were injured and even killed in the mayhem. I remember my former pastor told us of how he used to preach on the Berkeley University campus in California during those years. I was amazed as he told of the students' reaction to his preaching. He said one day the students almost choked him to death with a microphone cord that was connected to the mic he was using to preach with. Eventually he was beaten blind by members of the Hell's Angels motorcycle gang as he preached about the love of God and he spoke of the hypocrisy of students who said they wanted peace, but seemed to seethe with hatred against the Prince of Peace, Jesus Christ.

He gave me a real insight into what was happening during that time and I can see now, how, though I was only a teen at that time, the culture was speaking to me and forming some of my ideas. I was not old enough to realize what was going on then, but now I look back and see how some of my thought processes were being formed. As I got older, the seeds that were sown during those early years started to sprout up and grow stronger in my later years.

The Vietnam War ended, and I was entering into my teen years with a different attitude. This new way of thinking was fueled with drugs, alcohol and a fresh wave of new "friends" who were also of the same mind set. Many were just experimenting, having fun and fitting in. Others were more serious about a lifestyle that seemed to lead to a utopia of peace and love. I was of the latter group. I was into a good time, for sure, but deeper in me was this desire for world peace. Rebellion to authority was part of the act as well. After all, the older generation with their outdated beliefs were in the way of this "new" utopian thinking.

I think that seeing the protesters on TV defying authority in the streets during the war days set the stage for many of us to do the same. I wanted peace on earth but was confused on how to get it to happen. I seriously believed that if everyone would "just get stoned," it would solve all the problems that society had. There would be no more war or hatred, and a utopia would emerge and there would be peace on earth. At the time I could not have formulated the true foundational thoughts that were motivating me, but in hindsight this was it. Looking back, I can see that in fact this was the underlying belief that was compelling me to do many of the things that I did during those days. I had no signs of protest nor do I remember seeing anyone with these signs (except on TV) and consciously saying "yeah that's it." But inside me, this *was* it.

The drugs were the fuel that filled my heart along with the relationships that I had with the many like-minded "friends." I thought I was just having fun, but I was really confused both spiritually and philosophically. I recall the way I felt when I left the jock world (the sports-minded crowd) and connected with the freaks (the drug crowd). With my new friends I felt a new sense of freedom. We were beating the system (so we thought) and having a good time doing so. Every day, the bus would drop me off at the school and I would head toward the field next to the school building to meet up with my friends. We would talk and joke and decide whether we were going to go to school or not. Many times we would decide not to and we would proceed to the store and figure out what we would do.

Sometimes we would write fake excuses saying "my son has a doctor's appointment and he needs to leave at 9:30," for example. Sometimes the school would call, but there was no one home to get the calls, so I never got caught. We usually ended up at someone's house or, if it was warm enough, the woods, to drink, smoke and do drugs. I do not recall ever being confronted by anyone. The fact that I was not confronted left me continuing to spiral out of control.

The years in high school passed with parties and little involvement in the academic side of things. I remember my hockey coach asking a friend of mine, Mike D., how he was doing academically. He responded by asking, "What's that?" Mike influenced my life in a strong way, in the wrong way. He was an inner-city guy that was bused in during the days when the government wanted to integrate blacks and whites. He was a white guy, and as a guy who was raised in the city, he was streetwise and into many corrupt things. He taught my other suburban friends and me how to party in a way that I didn't know existed.

The goal of all get-togethers was to get as "blasted" as possible. There were no boundaries and nothing was wrong, as long as it pushed you to the goal of "getting wasted." Mike had great potential as a hockey player but his attitude and his unwillingness to discipline himself led to his destruction. Most of the team was competing to see who could ingest the most alcohol and drugs. Everyone in my sphere to one degree or another was doing it, there was no one I can think of who did not party at some level. Something inside was telling me that this was not right, but the culture was drowning out the voice of my conscience. I heard no external voices condemning this action. There probably were voices, but I was not hearing them.

The spiral continued as I found that getting wasted was a lot of fun. One day, my mom found a quarter pound of marijuana in one of my dresser drawers. She asked me what it was, and I told her. She seemed upset and told me to get rid of it. My mom and dad would drink socially at night and as a result, in my mind, could not tell me to not drink or do drugs. My justification was that you can't demand someone else to do what you are not doing yourself.

Parents have a hard job today, too, as kids are faced with peer pressure from every angle. Sometimes kids, will threaten that they will move away if they don't get their way which puts parents in a no-win situation. If I let the kid go what will happen, versus letting him get away with doing wrong under my roof. It's a tough situation. Things have really not changed all that much. Again this was indicative of the times, where the prevailing philosophy was "do your own thing." In the Seventies, authors were writing books about child rearing basically saying, "hands off, let your child do what they want." My parents were good people, yet were not equipped to deal with the spiritual darkness that was influencing that generation. Like most parents during those days they simply did not get it and were not prepared for managing the rebellion and the influences of the counterculture.

Graduation from high school was getting closer, 1976, and one of the things my dad instilled in me was to make something of my life. As I got older my "if it feels good do it" mentality seemed to conflict with the "be a responsible human being" mind set. I thought about the military and believed that it would be the best thing for me. I could start fresh and get the discipline that I needed. My grades were not good enough for college, and I still had too much rebellion in me. I figured that the military would help me be more disciplined. I would find a marketable skill and be able to find a job or go to school when I got out. The Air force it was.

So, I signed up and would go the following fall, which would have been 1977. In the meantime, I planned to live it up until the day I left home. Parties, good times and rock and roll dominated my life. We graduated from the parties in the woods to the bars and clubs downtown. But, I began to realize that the utopian experience was not going to be achieved through the hippie life style and philosophy, when all my friends were getting into fights as a result of being intoxicated and high. I thought to myself, this philosophy doesn't work, because if it did there would be no fights, only peace and harmony. This philosophy, I determined, was flawed.

Knowing this still did not stop me from pursuing pleasure at all costs. After all, the thinking was, you only live once and if I died, oh well, I would just be gone, and that would be it, so what. Like the Apostle Paul said, "if Christ be not raised, we are all still dead in our sins, let us eat and drink and be merry, for tomorrow we die"(1Cor 15:32). So my friends and I continued to "party on."

One night a couple of my closest friends and I went into a local grocery store and decided to rip off some beer. We tried to hide the six-packs under our long coats. We thought we had the establishment fooled, until we were met outside the store by the police. They arrested us, and suddenly our fun had come to an abrupt end. We were in trouble. Big trouble.

Chapter Two

Things Were Changing

I remember being really upset after the arrest and wondered what was going to happen. I went to the court hearing, and the judge said that he would go easy on me since I was going to go into the military. But he said that he had better not see me again. I thought to myself that I had better be a little more low key until I was actually in the Air Force. I determined that I would be a little more careful and not quite as crazy.

I still was intent on doing what I wanted, though. The Bible would say that I was in gross darkness (Isaiah 60:2). I was really into dirt bikes, and at the time, I was riding in the woods and racing motocross. There was a field by my house where we used to ride, and by the motocross track there was a stream where we used to hang out. We would drink there, and after I was drunk I would get on the bike and ride.

One night after drinking and getting high, I got on my bike with my girlfriend on the back. We started down the track right next to the place we were drinking. It was pitch black out, and because it was a dirt bike, my motorcycle had no light. The next thing I know my girlfriend and I were in the field. We were hit head on by another dirt bike with no light. My girlfriend's leg was broken, and I had a concussion.

The Bible says that men love the darkness more than the light because their deeds are evil (John 3:19). This was me. When you're walking in darkness you never know what you're going to run into. Even though I was trying to be more low key, I still had an I-don't-care attitude. Many nights, I would ride my dirt bike home on the main roads totally intoxicated, and the noise would make the neighbors' windows shake.

After I graduated I worked for one of my dad's customers and was just biding my time until I joined the Air force. The summer of 1977 began, and I was set up to go to the Air Force that fall. Every Fourth of July there were field days at the plaza not far from my house. One night we were at the festivities, drinking and goofing off as usual. My buddy asked me if I could give him a ride home. At the time I was riding my 250 Yamaha and was always into riding, anytime, anywhere. So he hopped on, and in my drunken and stoned stupor, off we went.

I managed to get him home safely but on my way back, while pulling into the plaza parking lot, I noticed flashing lights behind me. I stopped, and the officer approached me and asked me to get off the bike. I didn't think I was that drunk, but when I was getting off the bike I almost fell down. They did some roadside sobriety tests to determine if I was intoxicated. They told me to lean my head back and touch my nose. I failed that test. Then they asked me to walk a straight line. I couldn't do that either. I remember it like it was yesterday. They frisked me and, fortunately for me, they did not find the pot I had in my pocket. I think they were looking for weapons. They proceeded to put the cuffs on me and take me to the station. I pleaded with them to let me go because I was going to the Air Force, and I felt at the time that this would prevent me from going. They didn't listen. They wrote out five tickets including speeding, driving while intoxicated (DWI), and driving with no insurance, license or registration. I sat at the station until the wee hours of the morning waiting for my dad came down to pick me up.

The next day my dad had a talk with me. I honestly do not remember it. Inside, I was coming apart, wondering, why is this happening? My younger sister had become a Christian about a year before this, and I knew that something was going on with her, but I was not up to speed at all in terms of anything spiritual. I walked in on a Bible study at the house once, but didn't understand how Someone dying on a cross a long time ago had any relevance to me personally. That night, though, I got up on the roof of my house to watch the fireworks coming from the plaza, and I looked up at the stars and said, "Lord, if You are up there and You care like people say, please help me." I didn't have a "spiritual experience," but for the first time in my life that I could recall, I noticed the awesomeness of the stars and the thought of a God who loved me really began to speak to me. This happened about a month before my next trial. I laid low and remembered that experience on the roof.

The time for the trial arrived, and I stood before the same judge I had stood before a few months earlier on the stealing charge. I really thought that he would throw the book at me. But he didn't. He dismissed the three lesser tickets and reduced the DWI to DWAI (driving while ability impaired), which meant I had to attend Alcoholics Anonymous meetings, my license was revoked for a year, and I received a $25.00 fine for the speeding ticket. I couldn't believe it.

I left the courthouse, and something happened inside me. God had heard me. I know many would say this is all coincidence, but God was speaking in my language. To this day I don't know why the judge did what he did, but I know it was an answer to my prayer. Inside me, things seemed different. My friends asked me what happened–they had no clue what was going on inside me. I tried to explain without sounding stupid, that I felt that God had helped me. They did not get it at all. All I knew was that *something* was different.

I started reading the Bible and going to my sister's Bible studies. The more I read and listened, the more I realized that I had to make a choice to follow God totally. I began to notice a great conflict inside me. Part of me wanted God and knew He had a plan for me that was good. The other part of me was in stark rebellion to this and was unwilling to surrender to

Him. What I would call the "Romans 7 conflict" was going on inside me. The Apostle Paul wrote, "I was alive without the law but when the commandment came sin revived and I died" (Rom. 7:9). Prior to this courthouse experience I had no consciousness of God at all. But now I did, and with this new sense of God, I also had a new sense that something inside me yelled a huge "no" to Him. Paul also said, "But it is no longer I who do it but sin that dwells in me"(Rom. 7:17). It is like you're speeding down the Autobahn, where there is no speed limit, and all of a sudden, you see a sign that says fifty miles an hour. Automatically you say, "Who put that sign there? I'm not obeying that!" You question the authority and refuse in your heart to do what it says. That is what was happening to me. I was beginning to realize a Higher Authority, and something inside was saying "no."

I told my sister one day that I felt God wanted me to teach the Bible, but I was not going to do it. I figured that I would just read the Bible every so often but not be totally committed. I was on a roller coaster: one day I would be reading the Bible, the next day I would be out with my friends, getting wasted. Deep down, I knew I needed to give my life over totally but felt unable and unwilling to do so. I began to see that I was in rebellion to my Creator and not just having fun.

Some people wonder when a person is converted. What I was experiencing was not conversion, but the beginning of enlightenment. I was beginning to see things and understanding was coming to me, but I was not surrendered to His Lordship. I was in great turmoil. When I read Romans 7, I can see my struggle in that chapter. I found in me a desire to do good, but the power to do right was not there (Rom. 7:18-19). I was gaining an understanding and things were getting clearer, but I still was unwilling to surrender totally to God. This conflict went on inside me for about a month. I had pretty much determined that I was going to do my own thing despite God's help to me in the courthouse and despite the understanding of Him that I was getting through His Word.

Around this time, there was a rock concert in Buffalo, New York featuring Lynyrd Skynyrd, Yes, Ted Nugent and Bob Seger. My friend drove, and on our way we took some LSD. By the time we got to the concert we were all tripping. LSD puts you into a different level of consciousness. Things that don't move begin to move. Colors are different and everything is funny, unless you're on a bad trip or, in my case, running from the "hound of heaven," a reference to God's Spirit. As the concert rolled on, I proceeded to take more drugs. I believe the Spirit of the Lord was convicting me, and I felt very guilty about what I was doing. I was literally trying to drown out the intense feelings of conviction that I was experiencing.

While I was at the concert walking around I looked down and, there, with his back against the wall sitting on the turf of the Buffalo Bills'stadium, was my neighbor, Tom L., who was the same guy that was instrumental in leading me down the wrong road when I was real young. He was trying to get the last hit off a joint that looked like it had burned out ten minutes earlier. I was appalled, and the Spirit of God opened my eyes to the loss and desperate condition of this guy and deep inside I thought, "I do not want to be like him."

Yet, in reality, I was just like him. I wanted more for my life than what I was doing, and somehow, I knew that only the Lord could help me accomplish more. The conviction of the Holy Spirit shakes you about guilt and Hell, but He also shows you what you are missing and the life you could have with Him.

It was not about pleasing society or giving in to the establishment any more, it was about making my life count and fulfilling the purpose for my life. I believe the Spirit of God is the strongest force on the planet, though He is not just a force, but God Himself. He can break through any darkness, anytime. That's why I never judge a person on the basis of his outward behavior because no matter how it looks on the outside, that person may be ready to accept the Lord.

God was truly convicting me deeply, and while we were walking around the stadium my friend asked me about this Jesus I had been talking about. I was so disturbed inside I told him to shut up. I did not want to even hear that name. Even when I would hear the name of Jesus taken in vain I would shudder. Words fall short to describe what I was feeling. My soul was being cut to the quick; there was a deep piercing inside. No doubt I was troubled, but now I really was seeing it in the light of eternity. I always just thought that doing my own thing was just me having fun. After all no one was getting hurt, a common defense for doing wrong. I really started to see my behavior in the light of God's Law.

Up until the time I started going to Bible studies with my sister, I don't remember hearing a single sermon about God's Law, the consequences of violating that law or what Hell was. But now my inward eyes were being opened to these things. "When He comes, He will convict the world [the unsaved] of sin [what it is], of righteousness [God's Law] and judgment [eternal consequences]" (John 16:8-11). And that was exactly what was happening. The word convict means to "cause to see," to open your inward eyes. I started to feel detached from reality and felt that I was going to be separated from God, by going to Hell forever. All this was internal. There was no preacher or any outward voice, it was all inside me. Whatever drug anyone gave me that day I took. I was trying to destroy the guilt and really didn't care how. It felt like I wanted to just die and for it to be over, but now I was afraid of a real Hell.

At the concert, I was hallucinating and saw things that were not there. Timothy Leary taught in the Sixties that LSD really opens your mind to what is already in the unseen world. The Bible talks about the unseen or the spiritual world in descriptive language: angels, demons and spiritual forces of wickedness in high places (Eph. 6:10-12). There was a war going on for my soul. The power of sin and evil wanted to trap me in its web, and the very thing I wanted to do, that I knew was right to do, I was not doing, but I was doing the thing that I did not want to do (Rom.7:19). God's word was making me see the real, but I was still bent on the counterfeit. Many today are in the valley of decision on one level or another. The Holy Spirit is still working His work, how and at what level and with whom I do not know, but I really believe He is real and is working profoundly in the world today.

I had opened myself up to a demonic oppression that caused me to see a counterfeit of the real. Drugs are fun; there is no doubt about it, that's why people do them. "There is a way that seems right to a man, but its end is the way of death (Prov. 14:12). I tell people if it feels good before (thinking about it), during (that actual event), and after (how you truly feel about it when it's all done), then it is probably something that is okay, provided that your conscience is not totally seared.

And that is a problem. When people are not raised with any concept of God or absolute truth, they do not have a trained conscience or a Biblical world view. Even though Paul said that the Law is written on the heart and everyone inwardly knows there is a God, he also says men's consciences can be dulled or seared (Rom.1:21, Titus 1:15-16). Therefore, like myself before my conversion, whatever felt good and was accepted by society (and even if it wasn't), that's what I would do. So my world view (there is no truth and life is to be lived for pleasure and whatever feels good do it) was motivating me along with a darkened mind that was not trained to see or understand a spiritual world.

The struggle was so intense that, even in a drug-induced state, I felt His hand and a strong feeling that

He was calling me to surrender. I fought the same feelings of conviction all the way home. The next morning, I woke up and was in my right mind. The drugs had worn off, though I really thought that I would never come down from the trip I was on. Some say it was just a bad trip, but I knew differently.

On my bed when I woke up I cried out to the Lord. I honestly did not think that He would forgive me, feeling like I gone too far in my rebellious activity, like an adulterer who was forgiven many times, only to go back to those lovers. But now it was real. I had no hidden agenda; I asked Him to forgive me and told Him I would do whatever He wanted me to do. At that moment, I sensed the peace of God filling me, and I knew that I was forgiven. God knows what we need and at the time that is what I needed. Romans 8:16 says, "His Spirit testified with our spirit that we are the sons of God." At that very moment everything I needed for life and Godliness was given in seed form and has been in motion until this day (2 Peter 1:2,3). Peace was what I was really looking for, and it came to me when I surrendered to Him. Jesus said, if you love your life you will lose it but if you lose your life for My sake you will find it (Matt 10:39). I can truly say I was apprehended by God. It was emotional and life-changing.

After my conversion experience that morning of August 20, 1977, Dan Mc., who was instrumental in my sister's conversion, came over to my house for no apparent reason. I think he was looking for my sister, but God sent him over to minister to me. I told him what happened, and he shared with me many

things about God and why I was feeli...
was. He was shocked and amazed at my sto..
to this day, I praise God for him. I would go to him
with many questions over the next few months, and
he was gracious in answering them.

One day I was asking Dan some questions, and
he looked at me and said, "Why don't you ask God?
Get on your knees with your Bible and ask Him." I
didn't know you could do that, so I started and found
that God would meet me and talk to me there in that
place. It really is a habit that I have kept up with
through the years. I try to encourage young people,
read your Bible and pray in the morning, it will
change your life and many of your questions will be
answered in time.

Chapter Three

Times of Transition

After I became a Christian, everything changed. I tried to tell my friends about Jesus, but they did not have "ears to hear." They thought I was off the deep end. I tried my best to explain to them what was happening, but they just didn't get it. So, sadly, our friendships were over. I tried for years to keep a connection without engaging in what they were doing, in terms of drinking and carousing, but my efforts were not reciprocated. I wrote letters from college, as I felt a strong burden for their souls, but they never wrote back. So finally I stopped writing. Paul wrote, "And what communion does light have with darkness?" (2 Cor. 6:14).

One of the things they did ask me, though, was "how do you know the God of the Bible is the real God?" This stuck with me, not because I doubted my experience, but because I wanted to be able to answer them. This is what motivated me to think about going to Bible college. In those early days my mind was open to the Word, and I read the New Testament over and over. At the time I was working for the water department and we would drive around doing service calls. While we would go from place to place (the senior would do the driving), I would read the New Testament. I would come home on my lunch break and watch Pat Robertson and the 700 Club. I was so amazed at the power of God to heal and the testimonies that were shared.

About six months after my salvation experience, I was able to lead a Bible study. Many good things were happening, and I was experiencing the presence of God in a strong way. Everywhere I went I felt that God was there and often I was able to testify to people. Even at the A.A. meetings I had to attend, I would tell the people about Jesus, saying, "He is the only one who can help you." (There was a lot of smoke in those A.A. meetings, but it wasn't the shekinah glory.) Before my conversion, I was never able to talk to others freely unless I was drunk or high, but now the Word of God flowed from me. As the Bible says, in Acts 4:31, when the Spirit came, the Apostles spoke the Word with boldness.

One of the things that became clear early on in my understanding was that if God was the God of all, then He knows all, and therefore, He knows what I should do with my life. All I needed to do was to walk with Him daily and ask Him which way I should go (Ps.32:8). That is really how I have lived from that point to this, and I still believe that God has a plan for each person, and it is a good plan (Jer. 29:11).

The plan of God is for now into eternity. The world is moving at breakneck speed. Technology is exploding, and as the Bible says, knowledge is increasing at an exponential rate. (Dan. 12:4). Yet God says the world by its wisdom did not know God (1Cor. 1:21). You cannot know God experientially by acquiring information. You can only experience Him by the supernatural work of the Spirit. I was very hungry for the truth. Jesus said, "I am the way, the truth, and the life" (John 14:6). Like David, I desired truth in my inmost being (Ps. 51:6). After my conversion, I spent a year at home then a door opened to a "Discipleship House" on the Syracuse University campus. Dr. Koshey was the pastor of the church on campus and he was the one overseeing the Discipleship Houses. They were designed to help young Christians to grow and become established in the faith. I lived with seven other guys in one house, and Koshey lived with his family next door. They were from India and so full of love and faith. I grew tremendously during those two years and thank God for the experience. I decided to put the Air Force on hold and never did go. I had such a hunger for truth and to study the Bible. Koshey had a desire to reach out to the international students, so we had a dinner once a month for them in our basement. I met so many from different countries; it was a real great experience. I really never thought much about people from other countries, but now my eyes were opened. I always wanted to tell them about Jesus, but Koshey believed in friendship evangelism. This has served him well through the years as many have been converted to the faith. At the time, I just wanted to know the Bible better.

This led me to think about Bible college. I talked to Dr. Koshey and Rich Dickenson, an associate pastor at Friendship Evangelism Assembly, and they counseled me to pray for a year and then see if I still had a desire to go. During the next year, I was working at a Honda car dealership in Syracuse, and my friend Bryant and I started a cleaning business which was doing quite well (we called it Resurrection Cleaning Service). Bryant and I grew up in the same area and had many of the same friends but I never really knew him growing up. We became Christians about the same time and he also came to the Discipleship House. We became good friends and remain so until this day. We were real excited about the things of God.

When you're first converted, you think that everyone should have the same type of experience. I met many who did not have the same experience. In fact I met many people who did not seem to be what I felt were true followers of the Lord. When I became a Christian, I thought that you had to give it all for Him, which I did and continue to do. I have become a lot less critical through the years, but I still believe that if you're going to believe, then go all the way. Jesus said, "deny yourself, take up your cross, and follow Me" (Matt. 16:24). However, people struggle in many ways, with many things, in our modern contemporary culture of easy pleasure. My own suffering both emotionally and physically has made me more sensitive to people. He is mindful that we are dust (Ps. 103:13-14). At the Discipleship House, I grew a great deal.

A year passed. My friend Bryant decided to go into the Air Force, and I decided that I still wanted to go to school, but I had no idea where I should go. I was in the Discipleship House which was a big old house with four floors; I was on the top floor praying and asking God about Bible schools. I had no idea how many Bible schools there were. Somehow, I had a *Campus Life* magazine that had many of the schools in it, and as I was turning the pages, I landed on the Toccoa Falls College ad. It was like the Spirit said this was it. I felt a strong sense of God's favor and direction to this place, though I knew nothing about it. My pastor, Dr. Koshey, encouraged me to go Columbia Bible College in South Carolina. He knew the president and thought it would be a good place. So my buddy Jim L. and I got in my yellow Mazda pickup and headed south, first to Toccoa, Georgia and then to Columbia, South Carolina.

The first thing I remember about Toccoa Falls College (TFC) was loud rock music blaring in the dorm. I thought the school was beautiful, but I was not impressed with the laxness of the control of the music. (Early on in your new life it seems that everything is sin. I'm not sure what music was playing, but at the time I felt troubled by it. Now I can listen to certain music without offense but then it was not the case.) My friend Jim was not impressed either.

We left there and headed to Columbia. This place was not as nice aesthetically, but it seemed more conservative, and the people were friendly.

ought through the decision, I felt that the
ning to do was to honor my pastor and go to
mbia. Convinced that this is what God wanted
me to do, I made plans to go to Columbia. I moved
out of the "D House" in August of 1980, and went
to my parent's house in West Bloomfield, Michigan
(about 20 miles north of Detroit). I was waiting for
a reply from Columbia. They finally called and said
that the school was full, and that there was simply no
room. I was upset because I really thought that this
was the place I was supposed to be. I prayed for a
long time and then called them again, and they said
the same thing.

I was at my dad's house and he was wondering
what was going on as I was making these calls and
going from room to room praying. Finally, I realized
that Columbia was not going to work, so I called
TFC. They were still in registration, and I talked
to the man I had met when I visited. He was a real
nice guy and said, "come on down." That was all I
needed. My dad helped me on the plane to Atlanta,
then I took a taxi to the train station. The train took
me to Toccoa and a taxi took me to the school. It took
about six hours. I was a little afraid, as I did not know
anyone, and it was a different place.

The amazing thing was that even though I tried
to go to a different place, God really wanted me at
Toccoa. The sense that I had when I saw the ad was
the Lord speaking to me. You may wonder about
your life what you should do, where you should go.
God will speak to you and make His will known. You
must be patient and open to His leading, but usually

the thing that you really want to do (within moral bounds) is God's will. Don't struggle like I did, but simply follow the inward leading, that comes from a relationship with God and His word, along with sound counsel from others you trust. God will confirm His direction for your life, and you will have a deep sense of peace. There will always be a little turmoil, like going from first to second grade but you will know that this is the next step.

At Toccoa, I was in a new place physically, and now I was also being challenged mentally and spiritually. At the D House, we had learned a great deal, and there was much stress on service to others, such as friendship evangelism to the students at Syracuse University and living with brothers in Christ, with a concentration in helping and serving each other. The college scene stressed learning and academics, not service. There were opportunities for service, but the main thrust of the school was preparation for future ministry.

My pastor told me before I left for college that I better beware, that not all students on a Christian campus were real Christians. I was determined that I would not be swallowed up with the mediocrity, so I spent much time in prayer and took long walks in the hills behind the school crying out to God for more of Him and to know the truth. The first week that I was at the school, I felt a burden to go uptown (about two miles from the school) and try to talk to someone about the Lord. I met Steve. He literally looked like a walking corpse. I think this was in part due to his physical make up and the other part his involvement with drugs. He listened, and we developed a relationship, though I think he wondered about me. Through the years, I would go to his home and talk to his family. They understood that I was a student and, being in the Bible belt, they knew that they were supposed to be Christians, but I don't know if they were or if they knew whether they were.

My classes were challenging the first year because I had not really developed any real study skills. In my "B.C." days, as I have mentioned, school was not high on the priority list. After my conversion, I read the Bible and other books and also took a class at the D House which was theological but never had any real requirements. There were no papers to do or homework that would actually be looked at. At TFC, I was taking third-year theology classes my first year, which was a mistake. I was spiritually ready but not mentally ready, like a young person who thinks he is stronger than he actually is. He goes in the gym ready to lift a large amount of weight but can't. He must start smaller. That's how it was for me. My desire was there but my mind was not strong enough; my ability was not there yet, but it was coming.

The burden of the Lord was so strong on me during those days, and I really wanted to reach out to the community. I met Rodger B., a Methodist pastor who had a similar burden for the town. We decided to start a coffee house ministry outreach for the kids on the street. While we looked for a place, I met a Christian brother at the school who invited me to his church which met in a house. Pastor George Wester was pastoring the church, and it seemed like

the people had a similar passion to reac[
the town.

One day on campus, I was talking to Chris Todd
and gave him a song sheet that I had from the church.
He must have been familiar with the songs and liked
them, because he asked me where the church was. I
told him, and he and his wife began to go. Chris and
I became fast friends and when Rodger and I found
a place for the coffee house, Chris and I painted
scripture on the outside of the building. Rodger did
not feel led to be a part of the ministry, but offered
support and we kept in close touch. The church began
to grow, and Chris and I met on the weekends to
pray and do what we could to reach out to the young
people that would hang out around the building.

We had an organized street preaching meeting
one week. We met in a parking lot behind a strip mall
plaza; many of the students from the school came
as well as the kids from the town. We had singing,
and I was able to preach. It seemed like there was a
good response, and many kids seemed to be encouraged, but later that night a kid was shot and died in
Chris' arms. The police found the guy that shot him,
and to my knowledge, he is still in jail. It was difficult to reach the town kids; we would talk to them
in their cars while they hung out in the parking lots.
They were either uninterested or they knew that they
needed to give themselves over to Him, but did not
want to. We never came with a heavy hand, just the
gospel of the death, burial and resurrection. Most
were raised in the church and were "gospel-hard-
ened." I was still new to all the Christian stuff and

didn't really understand people in the South. It was a totally different culture from what I was used to in the North. All I really knew was that I was delivered from a life of death and destruction, and I wanted others to have what I had.

The church continued to meet at George's house but eventually needed a bigger place, so we started meeting at the coffee house building. George and his wife were in transition in their life and felt led somewhere else, which created a vacuum in the pastoral position. As a relatively new Christian, I really was not aware that there was a vying for the pastoral position. I could not understand why people did not just want to win the lost. I see more now that true leadership is vital for the continuance of any true work for God, but then I really did not. Jerry was a friend of George, and I think he wanted the role of pastor, but Chris felt strongly that *he* should take over. I am not sure how, but Chris was installed as pastor, and the church grew and the outreach continued. Jerry didn't continue attending the church, and as much as Chris tried to reach out to him, he was not receptive.

I was a student, and I was working in the church and the outreach. I had to pay my own way through school, so I worked on campus, and as a result of my extracurricular activities, my grades suffered. As I look back, there were a lot of things I would do differently, but youthful zeal and a burden for the town was directing me. During this time, I was studying the Bible intensely through my classes and on my own. I would spend hours in the library working on papers and trying my best to read the books that were assigned and, at the same time, do what I felt led to do in regards to the church and outreach. It did not make sense to me to spend all this time reading about what we should do, but not do it. This was the beginning of my struggle between the knowing of and being committed to doctrine, and the experience and Charismatic expression of Christianity. Most of my professors were mainline (non-Charismatic) and, at the time, I did not really understand the depth of the conflict that was going on. I was just zealous to know God and win the lost. The people I was with seemed to feel the same. In reality there should be no conflict, but there was and is, and this conflict sent me into years of learning and seeking answers.

In 1979, two years after I became a Christian, I attended a Full Gospel Businessmen's meeting. All the people were speaking in tongues, and the main guy was praying like a mad man and "lengthening legs" (this is where the minister will take your feet in each hand, and your leg that is not the same length as the other will "supernaturally" lengthen). At the time, I did not know what to make of it. My friend who was with me began to speak in tongues, and I think I did a little, but it was not real to me. I was just doing it because everyone else was. They said you did not have the Spirit if you didn't speak in tongues. But I knew I had the Spirit the day I was saved because my life was changed. I wondered about the whole thing but didn't seek that anymore.

My pastor friend, Dwight, told me that this kind of thing was questionable, and that I should stick with what the Word said and my own experience. Most of my church friends in Toccoa spoke in tongues. I had some of the visiting preachers lay hands on me to receive this gift, but, for whatever reason, I was not able to. I continued in the frame of mind that, yes, it was scriptural, and no, I did not have this experience. In reality, it seemed strange that all these people were speaking in these unknown sounds that didn't make any sense. Paul talks about this by saying, "For he who speaks in a tongue does not speak to men but to God, for no one understands him; however, in the spirit he speaks mysteries" (1 Cor 14:2). I was intrigued by this in the Bible and was not offended by people doing it, but the personal experience eluded me.

Chapter Four

A Dramatic Encounter with the Spirit

In 1982, I was on my way up to visit my folks in Michigan for the summer. I drove a car that a student gave me; it was a 1966 Dodge Dart with a push-button transmission system. I was happy to have something to drive. On my way up to Michigan, I passed the World's Fair, in Knoxville, Tennessee. I remember as I was going past the city, I felt that I should go there and preach to the people there.

I had never done any street preaching before, so I was a little scared. In Toccoa, we would talk to people on the street and did have that one organized meeting, but we never did any actual street preaching like David Wilkerson did, for example. (David Wilkerson was a pastor who went to New York City and preached to gang members; as a result, "Teen Challenge" was born to help drug addicts get clean.

His book, *The Cross and the Switchblade* tells the
story.) I threw off the feeling that I should go and
headed to Michigan. I thought, I can't go there alone,
and besides I didn't have much money. I arrived at
my parent's house, and I really wanted to do something for God for the summer.

It just so happened that there was a letter from
Child Evangelism Fellowship at my mom and dad's
house. I'm not sure why it was sent, but the letter
indicated they were looking for people to help and
be a part of the ministry. I sent in the application,
but I did not send in the form that asked about the
speaking-in-tongues issue. I think it was asking what
your position was, whether you believed it or not.
I'm not sure why I did not send it; maybe it was
because of the conflict that was still going on inside
me. Anyway, they called me and said they were
looking for a hundred workers and had ninety-nine.
They asked if I wanted to come for two-weeks of
training at Calvin College and then spend the rest of
the summer reaching kids for Christ. I knew in my
heart that this was it; God was in this for me, so I
went to the college and for the first week it was great,
learning the various scriptures and preparing to reach
kids for Christ.

After the first week, the leaders brought me into
a room and asked me about the letter that I did not
send, and what my position on tongues was. I told
them that I did not speak in tongues, but could not
deny that it was in the Bible, and they said, on that
basis, they could not keep me. I was devastated, and
I left the campus feeling totally dejected. While I was

driving toward my parents' home, the Lord reminded me of the World's Fair in Knoxville, so I turned the 66 Dart south toward Knoxville. I was scared, but felt that God was with me in a special way.

While I was at home, before I went to Calvin to prepare for Child Evangelism, I began to listen to some tapes by Pat Robertson. He was saying that you needed to be open to the gifts of the Spirit. I respected him, so my heart was a little more open to that dimension of the Holy Spirit. The Full Gospel Businessmen's meeting had put in me a negative mind set about tongues and that whole dimension of the Christian experience. Even though I was around it at my church in Toccoa, I still was skeptical. I was thinking about this on my way to Knoxville. I was out on a limb for sure now. I had very little money, had never spoken in the open air and did not know anyone in Knoxville. My spirit was crying out for help.

When I got to the city, the Devil asked me, "How are you going to survive down here?" (I know it was the Devil because of the doubt and fear in the suggestion. Whenever a thought or suggestion comes to your mind or heart and it makes you afraid or doubtful, it is the enemy of your soul.) I thought, man, you're right, I have to do something. I saw a sign that said you could give blood and earn money. So I walked to the hospital to give blood, but inside the hospital I had no peace, my soul was totally restless. I filled out all the papers, and as I was lying on a bed ready to give blood, I started to think to myself that this is not why I came here, and if God wants me to be here, then He will take care of me. Faith and restlessness were stirring in me, so I left. As I walked down the sidewalk the Devil spoke to me again the same thing: "What are you going to do, how are you going to make if financially?"

Vexed and troubled, I turned and went back in. This is a lesson to take to heart. If God has told you to do something, then He will take care of you. "God's work never lacks God's supply," said Hudson Taylor, who was a missionary to China. When I went back into the hospital, they told me because I had left the building that I had to fill out the forms again. At that point I said, forget that, and walked out of the hospital and up to a street corner and started preaching to the many that were walking by into the fair. Out of the corner of my eye, I noticed two men who were sitting on the corner listening to me. I kept preaching for a while and felt God's hand on me. I just quoted Scripture and tried to persuade people to believe. When I was done, the one man came up to me and told me that he was able to pray with the man that he was sitting with and that man gave his life to the Lord. I was so happy.

"Brother Bryant" was the man who prayed with the other man, and he invited me to his home that night for a prayer meeting. So I checked my schedule, and thought, hmmm, yeah, I guess I can go. So I went to his home, and he fed me and asked me if I had totally committed myself to the Lord. I thought, what I would be doing here if I was not fully committed? I told him my story, and we ate, and then some people started coming to the house for the meeting. I slept through the meeting, but at the end they were praying for people, and when he prayed for me, I started to speak in tongues. When I look back I can see how I was being prepared for this moment. We can't receive things from God until we are ready, whether it's salvation or any other gift that God wants to give us. We must be prepared.

I was in a position to receive and my heart was totally open. Before this, I could not receive the gift because of a mental block, a bad experience, or just that speaking in tongues did not make sense to me. But now, mentally and physically, I was ready. I sensed a new power in my life and would pray in the Spirit while I went to the fair each day (1 Cor. 14:4). The day after the experience, I met a man who had listened to me speak at the fair. He questioned me about the Holy Spirit and speaking in tongues. We read 1 Corinthians 14, and it was clear to me that speaking in tongues was for today, and that it was a blessing available to all who wanted it.

"I wish that you all spoke in tongues," Paul said (1 Cor. 14:5). The tongues in Acts 2:5-11 are known languages, but in Acts 10:44-48 and 19:1-6, the tongues may be the same tongues as in 1 Corinthians 12:7-11 and 14:2-40, which are unknown languages. I do not condemn any who do not speak in tongues and do not believe that they are not saved if they don't, but, like Paul, I wish that they all did for their own good. "He who speaks in an unknown tongue edifies himself" (1Cor. 14:4). What a divisive issue this has become, between those who condemn speaking in tongues and those who flaunt it! Paul lays out rules for tongues in the church. Sadly, these are not followed by most Pentecostal groups to this day.

I believe God sent me to Knoxville to receive the Spirit's manifestation of this gift. I was at the fair for about two weeks. I was able to stay with Brother and Sister Bryant; they took care of me and were a tremendous blessing. Even though they were not formerly educated they knew God deeply. I left Knoxville and was able to work with Youth for Christ for the rest of the summer. I did, and do, sense God in a stronger way and encourage all to receive and pray in the Holy Spirit.

When I came back to the campus that fall, I told the students of my experience and only one girl seemed blessed at all. I thought they would all be happy, but they were not. I commenced with school, church and outreach that year. Things seemed to be going well, my classes seemed good, and I was hungry for more. Evangelist Tom Allen came to the school and a revival broke out on the campus. Many were throwing their idols into the fire, literally, music and whatever else they were into that did not honor God. I remember riding past a fire on my way to the coffee house. It was amazing to see and hear that people were getting things right. I thought at the time that the Christians should be trying to reach street people and if they were really right with God they would. Now, however, I wish I would have stayed and prayed with the people that were making it right and then encouraged them to go out with me. Not everyone is called to reach street people but everyone is called to reach someone. Since that time many people did come out with me and showed a great deal of heart for the lost. The Christian service part of the curriculum that had only been tolerated by many was now embraced by the students as a way to reach out. The Lord showed up in a strong way.

Things continued to grow and develop at the church. A prophet came, and he prophesied over the people. Through his ministry, I received a great "word" that I have written down to this day. By a "word," I mean a statement about the person being spoken over that encourages them specifically or warns them of what may come. The intention is to instruct and challenge the person. The person speaking over the other does not know the person or his or her past, and yet in this case he was right on, specifically pointing out various struggles and challenges that each person had. It was amazing to see this guy in action. Every word was right on, and I was convinced that this was an authentic gift.

Chris was taking his place as the pastor. I remember the Devil speaking to me saying, "Who does this guy think he is? You should be the pastor." At the time, I struggled because I did want to preach, but I was not called to pastor that church. In fact, I had no real desire to pastor the church. I cast down those thoughts and tried to support Chris as much as I could, and he and his family supported me too. You may feel a call to do something that someone is doing, and it may be an authentic call, but the time and the place is not set, but it will be. Wait on God and commit to a life of prayer and study and God will make sure you find your place.

One time I was sick to the point of dying, and Chris prayed for me and I was healed. Sue, his wife, and Dax and Brandy, their kids, were my family in Toccoa. Chris and I worked together to reach the lost. God put the African-American people on my heart, and he and I would go to the bars where they would hang out. Sometimes we would go inside the bars and talk to them, but most of the time we would talk to them outside. I remember one day I was out with some folks from the church witnessing to the African-American people in front of the bar. I had been reading David Wilkerson's book *The Cross and the Switchblade*, and in one part of the book, Nicky Cruz, a gang member, tells David Wilkerson, who was street preaching at the time that he was going to chop him up into a million pieces. David's response was essentially, "if you do, every piece would cry out to you that I love you Nicky." This was what led to Cruz's conversion and a ministry that is still going, (formerly called "Teen Challenge," now "World Challenge"). Wilkerson's comment challenged me, and I thought to myself, could I do that? I didn't realize that I would be tested so soon, but on the street that night, a man pulled a knife out and told me he was going to "poke my eyes out." I hesitated some but said to him that if he did, I would stand there with no eyes and still love him. He stood there for a second and stared at me and then cut the gospel tracts that I held in my hands in half and walked away. Amazingly, I saw him not long after that at the church that met on Sunday night on our campus.

Jeff Tatarsky, a brother on campus, becoming good friends, and we both want the African-American kids who lived in the We brought about thirty little black kids to th one Wednesday. The church was not ready for the "sudden growth." It was pretty funny walking past the five people who were there to the back room where we ministered to the kids. They were happy about it but didn't know how to respond to it. The leadership then thought the best thing was to try to reach them on a different day. We tried for a while, but we were not really ready either. We were glad to be able to sow some seed into them. One kid did come to church for a while, his name was Cedric. I'll never forget him singing one day in front of the whole church, "I don't believe He brought me this far to leave me." I was so blessed. We were just doing the great commission with no other agenda.

Another guy I met was Eddy Gordon, a student on campus. This guy was a fiery evangelist. He would pull over when he would see kids on the side of the road, get out of the car and lead them to Christ. He would give out tracts at gas stations. He was amazing. I started to do the same; when I would see some kids walking, I would stop my motorcycle and talk to them about the Lord. Many did pray, but I often wondered if they really meant it. I guess only God knows. So many things happened during those days that I think were pivotal in helping grow in the Lord. Biographies that I read, such as David Brainard, George Whitfield, St. Francis and many others, fed my hungry soul. I went for long walks in the hills and ran for miles, meditating on the things of God. I believe that God was helping me to grow in grace and in knowledge in those days. I really did not participate in many typical college things, like ball games, and other social activities. I felt like I was there for one reason: to grow in the Lord and to be used of Him.

Our church was still developing, and God was sending some good people to us. Fred and Donna H. came and they added a strong prophetic dimension to the services. They both spoke the Word of God boldly. When I was getting ready to make poverty and a celibacy vow, Donna approached me and told me she felt that God was going to lead me into marriage and prosper me. I told her that was the opposite of what I was thinking. She didn't try to force it but just told me what she thought. You may wonder about these things, as I did, also. Generally, if someone speaks a word "from God," it will only confirm what God has already been speaking to you. Many times zealous Christians will speak wrongly to someone about important matters, and if they are young believers they will end up being vexed by this "word." Some have married the wrong person because they received a "word" to do so. God will not force you to do something against your will; He will give you the will, love or desire. "He is at work both to will and work for His good pleasure" (Phil. 3:12-13).

Fred and Donna were being used greatly but after a while things seemed to get out of control, in my estimation. I remember going to a "home group," and Donna was praying the blood of Jesus over and over

and weird stuff was going on. I realize that intercession is real and God looks at the heart, but at the time
this is what I was thinking. Again, I truly believe there
is a spirit of intercession, but the endless chanting the
name of Jesus, in my estimation, is not Biblical. These
abuses set me up for my later deep doubts about the
whole "Charismatic" thing. I was beginning to be
turned off to it all, but I still remained a part of the
church, and it seemed there was a strong "anointing"
on the work and the people really loved God (by
"anointing," I mean a real sense of God's presence).
There are no perfect churches and sometimes when
a work first starts, there are some abuses. Some are
from wrong motives and others are just immaturity.
Like Herod who wanted to kill Jesus when He was
a child (Matt. 2:16), so the enemy wants to destroy a
work of God before it gets strong.

We moved from the original coffee house to
another building that was better suited for the growth
that was happening. The outreach remained, though
the results were minimal if not nonexistent. One of
the benefits that I saw in it was being able to take
people from the school out and to expose them to
street ministry. Many of the students who attended
the school were raised in Christian homes and had
no concept of sharing their faith; to their credit many
did come out and were involved. Vinny was from the
Bronx, and one day in the Burger King parking lot
while talking to a bunch of kids, a kid hit him and
he looked up at me and said, "Did you see that?" At
the time I was talking to some other guys and did
not see what happened. I guess he told the people he

was talking to that they were going to Hell if they did not repent. He was a great guy and is now, to my knowledge, pastoring a church. The experience would stay with them the rest of their lives. This was my dilemma then, zeal for the Lord and evangelism on one hand and wanting sound doctrine and proper experience on the other. The college was providing a solid Biblical foundation, and the church was providing a fresh experience and powerful anointing and avenue for outreach and ministry. But the questions still lingered and would resurface later on.

Jeff and I became prayer partners during my last two years of school. Jeff was a Navy man who had an awesome testimony similar to mine. He became my closest friend, and remains so to this day. After the crash, he came up from Atlanta to Detroit and gave me a rock from one of the "witness heaps" where we used to pray. These were heaps of rocks we would set up like Abraham as altars or memorials of a place of encounter with God (Gen. 12:7,13:4-18, 31:45-49). There was a message of encouragement from him and his kids written on this rock, and it really helped me in my desperate hour. If there is one person who has influenced me the most, it would be him. One man said, "Leadership is influence; nothing more, nothing less, and nothing else." God used our relationship and it has given strength to both of us.

We would pray every day during lunch time on a rock near the school. When we first met, we would go for long walks to a rock near a stream up above the falls. It was about a two mile walk, and both of us felt like we were really pleasing God by taking this long walk to go and pray. At the rock by the stream we started praying for a revival and for many different people, when we were done, we got up and saw the imprint of our bodies on the rock. Our sweat left a print of our bodies. We felt good about our prayers. As time went along we got a greater revelation of God's grace. We began to realize that it was not our long walks that pleased God or got His attention, but it was, and will always be, the work of the cross. This teaching is so important because it focuses on God and not man. Modern Christianity seems like it wants to take God off His throne and put in the work of man "Look at what we have done. Look at our imprints." It is really an insult to Christ who bore our own sins in His body on the tree (1Peter 2:21-25). Prayer and preaching are catalysts to bring us to the throne room to receive the fullness of Him, all that He is in His beauty and power (Eph. 3:14-21). We should feel good about doing God's work and when it's done in His way, a true blessing does come to us, but it's not about our glory. No flesh should glory in His presence (1Cor. 1:31).

Jeff also started going to the church (which became Toccoa Christian Fellowship) and became a friend and a support to Chris. The three of us became close and worked together to build the church. One spring break, Jeff and I went to the beaches of Florida and preached to the people on the beach. We came to this one group of "twenty-somethings" (which is what we were at the time), and at about ten in the morning, they were almost totally drunk. A girl took our banner that said "Repent for the

Kingdom of God is at Hand," and started heading for the water. She walked about two hundred feet until she was waist deep and threw the banner into the ocean. She was mumbling something about being sacrilegious. I went out and retrieved it, and after a while, it dried off. We talked to the small crowd a little but they were not in a position to receive. All week we preached during the day and prayed at night. We slept by the ocean in his car that had real comfortable seats. The time was refreshing, and many people heard the Word. I remember feeling such a strong blessing on my life. I felt like I was doing what I was supposed to do.

On our way back to school in 1984, we wanted to fast and pray before the school year. In Tennessee, we pulled into this area to park by a lake and hiked down this trail to the lake. The lake was beautiful like a sea of glass. There were burned-down trees in the area that we ended up in. We never went for the long walk around the lake because we wanted to conserve our energy, but we did go for a swim. We spent a few days there, baking in the sun and consuming the rest of our gallons of water. When you fast you are supposed to sip water because your body needs to gradually cleanse itself and not wash out too quickly, because it washes your energy also. I think one of our goals in our fast was to get closer to God, as well as to entrust the school year to Him. The fast got off to a grueling start but we were determined to fulfill God's will in this endeavor. Anyway, we dragged ourselves out of there and went to George Wester's cabin. The cabin was not far from the school and was perfect for being alone with God. We spent some days there, and then I felt like it was time for me to end the fast. We went to church that Sunday morning, and I began to eat after that but Jeff still kept fasting. I used to worry about him; though he was bigger than me, still I was concerned. Later he told me that God had convicted him for trying to outdo me. It wasn't long after that, that he started eating. I guess he was still learning grace.

All these things really helped my experience with God. When you're a young, zealous believer you do things because you just feel compelled to. Like a little kid that only wants to please his parents: "Look at me, Daddy!" (Too bad they don't stay that way.) That's why the grace package is so hard to get. We are told from an early age, whether verbal or nonverbal, that to get anywhere or to please your boss or parents you will have to "make every effort." We translate this to our relationship to God. We really think that somehow after we are saved by grace we can please God by works. Read Galatians. The believers there were going back under the Law after being saved by grace. We gentiles don't have the Law of Moses, but we have our cultural expectations and "rules." The Christian world has its rules also. Different churches have different rules, but none of these rules, if obeyed, whether religious or secular, will bring anyone closer to God. No doubt they may make you feel good about yourself because you did these things, but as far as bringing you into God's favor they are powerless. This is not to say that you can live any way you want because you're "under grace." On the contrary, the grace of God teaches us to deny ungodliness and worldly lust and to live soberly (Titus 2:11-14).

Chapter Five

The "Seduction of Christianity"

I tell this story in order to set the stage for the coming bombshells that were going to challenge my mind. I was continuing to study, pray and work. The church was growing, and I was preaching once a month and was considered an associate pastor. The book *The Seduction of Christianity* by Dave Hunt and T.A. McMahon had been released, and it caused no small stir. As I read it, I thought that we at the church were all deceived and we had slipped into severe error and I needed to do something, but I didn't know what. Again, at the time, I was really seeking the truth, I wanted to be right and not fall into deception. This is a basic desire within all believers, a desire for truth and a fear of being wrong. Hunt and McMahon write:

Transcendentalism helped spawn what became known as New Thought, which emphasized that thought controls everything. The power of thinking, whether negative or positive, was believed to be sufficient even to create physical reality or to destroy it. God was not personal, but a great Mind which was activated by our thoughts and would actualize them into concrete form. The corollary to this axiom is obvious: man is divine. Forced out of the church at this time as heresy, New Thought became the basis for such mind-science cults as Christian Science, Religious Science, and Unity. Today's church is being swept by a revival of New Thought, now called Positive Thinking, Possibility thinking, Positive Confession, Positive Mental Attitude, and Inner Healing. We are very concerned that at this time New Thought, which represents inside the church what New Age is in the secular world, will not be forced out, but will remain within the evangelical church to contribute to the growing confusion and seduction. One of the most basic New Thought techniques is visualization, which is now firmly entrenched within the church.

He goes on to say, "While it is true that our thoughts influence us in many ways, it is not true that 'thinking,' 'speaking' and 'visualizing' contain the virtually unlimited power attributed to them; nor are they biblical methods for 'releasing God's power.' Mind manipulating techniques for solving human problems and creating health and wealth have always been part of the occult." This is just a small example or where he was coming from.

When I would come to visit my family in West Bloomfield, Michigan, I attended Bloomfield Hills Christian Church, which met in a banquet hall in Bloomfield. It was similar to our church in Toccoa, but it was bigger. I remember feeling a strong presence of God there, but there also seemed like there were some abuses. Women would be dancing wildly and the worship services seemed to be on the border of absurd. (Again, this is how I perceived it at the time.) But I have to say that I truly sensed the power of God. It was like our church in Toccoa times ten.

I couldn't get away from the desire in my heart for the real Christian experience and sound Biblical doctrine. I never sensed anything that was doctrinally questionable in these two churches but the book *The Seduction of Christianity* gave the impression that the Charismatic expression was completely wrong no matter what. I continued to go to the Charismatic churches but the controversy still remained, and in my quiet moments, I would ponder the position of Dave Hunt and the points that he made that seemed to bring into question the reality of the Charismatic experience. (I use the term "Charismatic," recognizing it means different things to different people, but its basic premise is a belief in the gifts of the Holy Spirit listed in 1 Corinthians 12, a strong emphasis on physical and spiritual healing, personal prophecies and hearing God's voice in dreams and visions as indicated in Acts 2.)

Everyone wants to be right and at Bible school that seemed to be what it was about, being right. One day there was a symposium at the school about infant baptism and many well-educated people were there stating their positions. At the time I thought, what does this have to do with salvation? People are perishing and they are talking about infant baptism. This was a total waste of time, I thought. But this is what school is about and it's good as long as you remember the purpose of why you are there, but in my estimation many forgot the central reason that they came to a Bible school. It's amazing how many traps you can fall into even at a Christian school. This heart-and-mind battle increased the more I studied and went to church. As I read Hunt and McMahon's work and mirrored it against where I was going, I could see what they were saying, and yet it seemed like there had to be a balance. Could we all be deceived? And what about these doctrinally accurate churches, they seemed so dead. My spirit wanted depth of feeling, not just emotionalism; it goes beyond that, it is a depth of an experience with the God who is real and active, not just words on a page.

I don't know Hunt or McMahon nor have I followed them through the years. I'm sure they have a lot of good things to say, but I needed to know the truth. Jesus said, "The hour has come where the Father seeks those who will worship Him in Spirit and truth" (John 4:22-23). Our minds need truth and our spirits need God. This began to teach me that you could not follow men. It is the Spirit that gives life; the flesh counts for nothing, Jesus said (John 6:63). The goal of us as Christians needs to be proper experience and proper apprehension of the truth. What is the truth? The pendulum swings back and forth in our day. Some on the Spirit side and others on the doctrine side, with very few in the middle. Some in Charismatic circles are always seeking experiences that would take them closer to God, while non-Charismatic believers do not focus on these, but rather what is written.

This explains the lack of true Bible study in many Charismatic churches while the focus is more on experience, though this is changing slowly. The Bible was written by Holy men who were "carried along" by the Holy Spirit (2 Peter 1:21). Men in whom God trusted to write His words. These men wrote the words they heard out of the experience they had with God. They were not in ivory towers but in prisons and in wildernesses. Thank God for all the modern conveniences, but somehow we need to enter an understanding of what was written in the spirit in which it was written. That means being alone with God and letting Him give us understanding by the Holy Spirit.

I loved studying the Bible, and I definitely saw a difference in those who were Spirit-filled and those who were not. There seemed to be a real excitement with the ones who were Spirit-filled verses a certain deadness among those who were not. At least that is how I was seeing it at the time. Only God knows the heart of each person, so I don't judge anymore, but at the time I was judging on the basis of what I believed at the time. At the time, though, it seemed to be an issue, and as I have walked this walk, I see it a little clearer and that is one of the things I really want to share. Many Spirit-filled Christians live compromised lives. Many "non-Spirit-filled" Christians live exemplary lives, but this distinction was raising questions in my mind about what was true.

On one hand I observed non-Spirit-filled Christians living exemplary lives and vice versa. I was trying to determine truth on the basis of someone's life. For example, this particular perspective must be more right because of how people were living it. But this is not wise. Paul said, "Let God be true and every man a liar" (Rom. 3:4). He also urged us to look to the Old Testament saints who through faith and patience inherited the promises (Heb. 6:11-12). People in every religion live lives that are morally pure in that they don't do any of the "bad stuff." But does this make them right? Christianity stands on its own as *the* Truth, regardless of whether anyone lives it. A person's life is their license to preach or talk to others; however the life and the message are two different things. For example, if a drunk on the street is preaching the true Gospel, his life does not nullify the truthfulness of the message; it is no less true regardless of his state of mind. No doubt our lives are watched and judged by others, and, as in the case of Jimmy Swaggart and Jim Baker, the message and the life behind it leave people wondering. However, this is part of the problem when the attention is on the messenger and not the message.

On campus, many saw and respected the work that we at the Church were doing, but some thought I was part of a cult and I tried to assure them that I was just like them. I would make an extra effort to make friends with the guys on campus, but I was not into a lot of the social events that brought many people together. In fact the more we prayed for revival, the more I became troubled about some of the things that were going on campus, like people taking pop out of the machine and not paying for it. A guy nick-named "Mad Dog" was also influencing so many in a negative way, there was excessive TV-watching, guys and girls seemed to be getting too close, some choices in music were questionable, and many other things deeply troubled me. One day, I went into the cafeteria and took the microphone that they used for announcements and told what was on my heart. I don't remember what I said, but the whole place became silent and listened to me. Many came after and said they appreciated the message. Another time in an open-mic chapel service, I stood up and told the students that what they did regarding the pop machine was a sin and they needed to repent. I did not thunder the word, but said it with broken heart. I'm not sure if they ever did get that right, but I just said what I felt led to say. Corruption troubles me even today. To see weak people trampled and bad people succeed at the expense of good people stirs me up inside.

I got together with a few of the brothers on campus and put together a skit for a chapel service. The skit was about a person who was being tempted to do wrong by the Devil, similar to the *Screwtape*

Letters by C.S. Lewis, in which the Devil was telling his demon to attack this particular person in various ways. It is an ingenious work, depicting how the enemy of our soul wants to trip us up and how we need to be equipped to deal with him. Paul said, "We wrestle not against flesh and blood, but against principalities and powers, spiritual forces of wickedness," and he goes on to tell the Ephesians to take up the full armor of God (Eph 6:10-20). Peter says, "your adversary, the Devil, prowls about like a roaring lion seeking whom he may devour" (1 Peter 5:8).

The skit was a great success, and I felt it really hit home to many people. It was such a blessing one of the actors in the play took the play to a missionary conference. I was glad that he did that but was really hurt that he didn't include me at all. He never talked to me about the whole situation. Now it seems foolish that I was so bent out of shape, but at the time it really upset me. I tried to release the whole thing as much as I could. I think God was saying, hey, whose glory are you seeking? Okay Lord, it's all in your hands. It's not easy to commit all things like that to God, but that is what needs to be done. It may take a while to get over what someone has done to you. Jesus said, "Bless those who curse you and pray for those who spitefully use you" (Matt. 5:43-44). This is one of the hardest things that Jesus asks of us, and it is really impossible to do it without His grace.

One night I felt the Lord tell me to go down to the town in front of the two bars where many African-American people hung out. A friend came with me, and we drove downtown and parked on the opposite side of the street in front of the bars. There were probably one hundred to one hundred-and-fifty people just talking, smoking, etc., in front of the two bars. We parked and headed across the street. They saw us coming, and just as if it were planned, half went into one building and the other half in the other. I stood and preached anyway. They knew me from coming down and talking to them on the weekends, but I guess that night they were not in a position to talk or hear. I really felt God's power and realized that, even with all my doubts, I could still follow the conviction of the Spirit, and He would be with me. Even though my theology may not be perfect, that was alright. Calling people to repentance and preaching the death, burial and resurrection of Jesus with the right intention is never wrong.

The early church fathers were not in agreement on all theological issues, and yet many of them died for the faith, preaching the death, burial and resurrection, and they loved God totally. God's Spirit is very strong, and there is balance to knowing and experience, feeling and thinking, soul and spirit. If you sit ten well-known preachers down and ask them theological questions you would get different answers. But at the time, I really wanted to be totally right, I didn't want to be speaking the wrong thing for the rest of my life. This is not a bad thing as long as you can come to certain conclusions, even if the conclusion is that there is no conclusion, but an open end. So much of theology is paradoxical and open-ended. Jesus said, "You have heard that it was said... but I say to you...." (Matt. 5:43-44). The people of Biblical times were no different than the people today, steeped in tradition and what they were taught from their fathers and culture. The Talmud was a Jewish commentary about the Old Testament and it had many opinions from men about the Law. Instead of looking at the Law and seeing their need for God, they made the Law more doable, filing down the edge of the sword, and making themselves more self-righteous. If man could do the Law, there would be no need for the God-man's death and resurrection for the sins of the world.

Today there is so much religion, but is there God's power? Where is the Lord God of Elijah, as one man asked, and then answered, he is waiting for Elijah to call on Him. "A broken and contrite heart, You will not despise" (Ps. 51:17). It's good to be doctrinally sound, and it is good to have a genuine Christian experience. When one source, like *The Seduction of Christianity*, makes broad statements, pointing out error, it may be good to examine one's thinking and be led into the Scriptures. But it may become a trap that Paul warned about in 1 Corinthians 3:4, "some say I am of Paul, Apollos and even Christ." The point is, you cannot base your faith on men or their opinions. Today, it is "I'm of Pastor So-and-So," or "I'm Catholic," or "I'm Baptist," and so on. A personal relationship with the God who created the world and sent His son to die cannot be based on anything that man says or is about. God uses people, but to put faith in frail humanity will never bring you to ultimate truth.

The Bereans in Acts 17:10-11, were more noble-minded than those in Thessalonica in that they "searched these things daily" to see if what Paul said was so. It takes a little time, but the investment is well worth it. Study the Scriptures in light of other Scriptures and what is known in the natural world and in your spiritual experience with God. What does it say (many times this may seem obvious, but doing word studies is a good thing, because the words that the writers used have definite meanings, therefore it is imperative to seek out the exact meaning of the words used and not pour our meaning into them), what did the writer intend, who was he addressing, what did he mean and how does it apply to me and my world, and then what should I do about it, if anything? It takes time and effort, much like digging for a buried treasure, but when the truth is found it is more precious than gold. Knowing these things made me realize that the responsibility was on *me* to find the truth.

Here, again, is the importance of hermeneutics, which is the art and science of Biblical interpretation. In some arenas of Christianity there is a thought that it is all God's Word, and if you pick up the Bible and read, it is like God talking to you. The thought goes that, if you're really "in tune," then there is no need to study or examine the texts, but rather just read, and God will illuminate you. This removes the work or effort it takes to study and focuses on feeling and hearing God. No doubt we need the Holy Spirit to help us in our understanding, but will it just come without really searching and using the brain that God has given us? Like the one man who desperately wanted to hear God so he opened the Bible and put his finger on a passage, "Judas went out and hung himself." He thought, "That can't be God," so he opened to another passage and put his finger on a verse, "Go and do likewise." Disturbed by what he read, he tried once more, "What thou doest, do quickly" It's a humorous story, but sadly, this is how many try to hear God. The Bible says,"Line upon line and precept on precept" is the way of understanding (Is. 28:10).

The truth is the most important thing: "Let not mercy and truth forsake you," Solomon said (Prov. 3:3). And David said, "I desire truth in my inmost being" (Ps. 51:6). Jesus said, "I am the way and the truth and the life" (John 14:6). Pilate asked, "What is truth?" (John 18:38). In the preceding verse (John 18:37), Jesus is talking about His witness to the truth, indicating He is the Truth. The truth is in a Person, not merely a set of words. God made words like He made everything else, and these words paint pictures of what is. When one tells a story it is like taking a brush and painting a picture, but a story can be told as the truth or half-truths or lies.

Words can be manipulated to say anything and mean anything. This is why the atheist is an absurdity, because he uses words with general understandable meaning and rationality, that is reason and logic, to say there is no meaning or rationality or logic or a Creator. A good example is the statement "everything is relative." Well, if everything is relative, then that statement is relative and has no meaning. "There are no absolutes," one person says. Again, are you absolutely sure? That statement itself is an absolute statement; therefore, to say there are no absolutes is absurd. If we are to have a fair conversation about life and meaning, we have to at least agree that we can communicate with words that have definite meaning. Words have meaning because God *is* and He *created them*, so it is an absolute absurdity to use rational statements to say there is no rationality or truth.

The fact that your mind can even follow this line of reasoning proves that there are receptors in the brain that bring this understanding and a sense of what really is. The letter "A" is "A." It is true, letters make up words to propose a certain meaning intended by the author. Any author would be offended if he wrote something and it was misinterpreted by the reader, like a teenage girl getting a letter from her boyfriend and reading between the lines. For sure we need the Holy Spirit to give us understanding, but when a passage in the Bible makes sense, truly seek no other sense. To admit that there are truths and truthful statements, one would have to admit that those truths came from somewhere and not just nowhere. Order cannot come from chaos and disorder, just as a painting has a painter and a machine a builder and a reason or purpose for its existence. A watch does not evolve over time, but it comes out of the mind and heart of the person who thought about it and constructed it to tell time.

Each word of the Scriptures must be studied and understood in the light of its context. Words build on words, and though their meanings can change in a minor way from generation to generation (like the words "cool" or "hot"), the basic flow of communication is the same in all dialects. If that was not true then the United Nations could not understand one another. God saw the power of words at the tower of Babel and broke the languages up (Gen. 11:1-9). The meaning of words did not change, but the dialects did, therefore they could not understand each other. At Pentecost when the Holy Spirit fell the people heard the Apostles speaking, in their own languages, the wonderful works of God. The people at the tower had wrong motives wanting to build a tower for their own glory. God said, "Indeed the people are one and they all have one language, and this is what they begin to do; now nothing that they propose to do will be withheld from them" (Gen.11:6). The Lord gave them different languages, because he saw that a unified speech would unite them in a powerful way, and for these people it would be for the wrong reasons.

He united the people at Pentecost for the same reason. A united people speaking of the wonderful works of God would be a strong force for good and God's kingdom. Much confusion has come regarding unity. But when you think about it has much to do with words. When people disagree they use words to tell their side of the story, but unity based on simple natural agreement is not enough. Paul said, "Preserve the bond of unity in the bond of peace" (Eph. 4:3). The unity comes by the Spirit, and it needs to be preserved by speaking the truth in love and guarding against dividing people with wrong words. We can generate a certain kind of unity on the basis of natural agreement about a certain teaching or we can preserve what is already given by the Spirit of God (for example, the many in-house debates like tongues, Apostolic succession, prosperity, healing, end times and the many issues that seem to take front and center in peoples' thinking). Agreement on a certain teaching that does not build off the foundation of Christ and what he did causes people to follow men and their teaching. Paul said "keep in memory," the death, burial and resurrection of Christ which means never forgetting the foundation of the cross (1 Cor 15:1-4). He also said, "For I determined not to know anything among you except Jesus Christ and Him crucified" (1 Cor. 2:2).

The New Age trap that wants to build unity through mere agreement, yet without the foundation of the death, burial and resurrection of Jesus according to the Scriptures, is in total error. The Bible should be studied and read with a clear mind, taking context into consideration. We should not read into the text (this is called "isogete"), but take out of the text its intended meaning (this is called exegete). Preserving unity has to do with relationships within the Body and is vital for the growth of the church. When the central Truth is forsaken, that is, Jesus Christ and Him crucified, then it's all up for grabs in terms of what we agree on. Many people come together because they agree on a certain doctrine and this becomes the foundation of the church. It could be eternal security or a certain belief about the end times. This is a faulty foundation, though because the foundation that is to be laid is Jesus (1 Cor. 3:11).

Back in the early church the battle was similar to what it is today; the difference is that today there is a more widespread diversity within the Body. One town has numerous churches all seemingly going after the same God. Within local churches people disagree about the color of carpet to be installed. I heard of one church that split, literally. They took a chain saw and cut it down the middle because they disagreed about Adam having a bellybutton. It may be fun to think about whether Adam had a bellybutton, but what does it have to do with salvation? (I'm not sure if this story is totally true, though I heard it from a preacher. But even if it is not, it still illustrates the point and how far people will go in standing by their position.) The Mormons said all the churches were wrong so they made a new religion. Paul said, "Let each one of you look out not only for his own interests, but also the interests of others" (Phil. 2:4). When the foundation is solid and the church really seeks the welfare of one another, then the church will thrive. If we are all fixed in our desire to please the One who died for us and not just be "right" then we will experience more of His presence and the church will go forward.

Chapter Six

Graduation and Beyond

I finally graduated in 1985, broke and in debt, like most college graduates. I stayed in Toccoa and did odd jobs and lived in a trailer with my roommate Setiwan Widjah from Singapore. Set, as we used to call him, was also a graduate and was looking for some direction. If you don't have family or church support while going to college, it is very difficult to find a place after you graduate even though you have a degree. If you're in debt and don't really have good connections, you end up working at various jobs trying to make ends meet and pay off your debts. Good men sit under good professors for four, five, and sometimes six years, only to go out and find no place to transmit their knowledge and experience. This, along with wondering about marital relationships, becomes a real issue for many guys, whether they are American or international students.

I really think that schools need to do a better job helping students to find places, especially when it comes to ministry. So many end up doing jobs that they did not go to school for because they can't find a place. It works both ways, guys accepting various jobs offered that are not related to ministry or, as in my case, rejecting good jobs because of God's call on their lives (my dad's company would have hired me to possibly take over his job as a salesmen for LaFarge Cement). I remember thinking that I did not want to commit to a job that I would have to leave soon. I look back at that decision with a lot of regret. But, again, at the time, you're following your heart. You are under the impression that now because you have a degree that doors should be open; for many it did work that way, but not for me.

I struggled with the whole marriage thing, not knowing what to do. Although I had friends on campus that were girls, nothing was happening romantically. I dated a few but at the time I was so focused on God and what He wanted that I think I scared them off. Some I really liked, but they didn't like me and there were others who liked me, but the feelings were not mutual.

In 1984, I met Suzanne from New Castle, Pennsylvania. She was coming to a "campus preview" to see if she wanted to attend the college. When I met Suzanne, she seemed troubled about different things and I tried to minister to her. She seemed like a nice person, but I had no feelings for her. I had guarded my feelings ever since, early after my conversion, I told this one girl I thought we would be married one day. Later, while in college, I felt that I spoke to soon to her. When I was at school I lost track of her. I saw her once before I graduated and realized I had no feelings for her. So, with Suzanne, I was not going to even think along those lines unless I felt a total liberty in my spirit. We wrote letters for a year after the campus preview, and most of my letters were sermons from what God was teaching me. Nothing romantic, because there was nothing romantic going on in the relationship. I did not want to let on about any feelings and didn't really know if I had any.

Then, one night, I was going for my usual nightly prayer walks, and it came into my mind that I should consider Suzanne and to think more about God's direction in this matter. I was not thinking about the marriage thing at all, it just came to me. I remember standing in front of railroad tracks and two trains crossed in front of me. On one of the trains there were two engines and in this brief display I felt God was saying two things. One is, the tracks of our lives are set and if God intends two people's paths to cross, they will. The second is, two are better than one, two can pull more weight than one. Two engines can pull more cars than one. So, whatever God had planned for the future, two can pull more weight and it is a good thing. "He who finds a wife finds a good thing and receives favor from the Lord" (Prov. 18:22).

Suzanne came down about a month after that prayer walk, to preview the campus again the following year, but I think God had other plans. She looked different than what I remembered (totally gorgeous), and we met and talked that weekend. I took her up to "The Falls," and we talked about the future, and I told her about the call of God I felt on my life. I was challenging her to see if she was willing to go anywhere and do anything for God. She seemed pretty steadfast about me and seemed to share the burden I felt. I remember thinking, could this girl really like me this much, she doesn't even know me? We talked and prayed that weekend, and I invited her to come back for my graduation.

She went back home after the campus preview and then came back down for my graduation, and it was then I proposed and she accepted. I wondered about many things at the time, she was young and maybe too young. A friend of mine on campus was engaged to a younger girl, and it didn't seem to bother him. Most of my friends and my pastor seemed to be in agreement and were positive about the whole thing. I never wanted anything to come between God's will for my life, including a wife. After I proposed, I stayed in Toccoa, and she went back to Pennsylvania.

What I was learning was that God wants to give us gifts, both internal and external, but many times we are not in a position to receive them. I struggled so much with what Paul said about marriage: "For I wish that all men were even as I myself. But each one has his own gift from God...." (1Cor. 7:7). So when the gift came, I had to really be able to accept it from God and believe that it was okay. You may struggle with the whole marriage thing; I encourage you to pray about it, and if you have a desire to marry, believe that God will provide. If you have no desire to marry believe that God is in that too. You will be of great use to Him either way.

In February, after talking to Pastor Chris, I decided to move up to my folks' house in West Bloomfield, Michigan. I could be closer to Suzanne and get a job that would pay more than five dollars-an-hour to pay off my debts. So I did. When I arrived at my parents' house I became sick, and I slept for a month on and off. I had no energy, nobody really knew what it was, but after about a month I snapped out of it. I talked on and off to Suzanne and we talked about when we would get married.

When my energy came back, my dad was able to get me a job from a company that he sold cement to, Carlisimo Concrete Materials, which was a concrete block and pipe company. They made pipe and blocks for sewers, homes and buildings. I started out in the block part where we made and stacked block. It was hard, nasty work but I really liked it. I was so burnt out from school work; it felt good to do something physical. I worked twelve-hour days and started to make some good money.

One day this worker and I were on a block machine and he was disengaging a block that was stuck, when all of a sudden the machine started (he should have turned it off, but he didn't). It pinned him and crushed him. I ran away from this huge bar that was coming at me. The bar was supposed to push the large stacks of block out onto to rollers where it would be picked up. I jumped up on the stack of blocks that the bar was supposed to push. The bar would have pinned me against the stack of blocks, but I was able to beat it and jump out of the way. I think the reason I was able to avoid being smashed was because he stopped the machine when he was crushed by it. We thought he was dead and then someone called his name and he started talking and making jokes. It took a long time to get him out; he was really hurt bad but was not killed or paralyzed. I was able to visit him and went to his house and was able to talk to him about the Lord.

It was such a different world from college. The people were foul and vulgar, but I felt compassion in my heart for them. I worked there for about three months and then right before I got married I switched jobs. My dad got me another job driving a concrete mixing truck. It paid more, and I figured the sooner I got my bills paid the sooner I could get on with becoming a minister.

Right before I got married, I talked to the superintendent of the Christian and Missionary Alliance denomination in Pennsylvania. I was not as well-informed about the denomination as I am now. He asked me about my history and about the differences between the Alliance and the Assemblies of God. I said that I thought they were similar. He became quite excitable and rebuked me for my statement. I remember that I felt very upset at his lack of tact and my own ignorance of the differences between the two groups.

He seemed especially angered at the "Word of Faith" people, and mentioned Kenneth Hagin and Kenneth Copeland, two people I didn't know much about, as I had only listened to a couple of their tapes.

I disagree with some of their teaching but consider them to be within the boundaries of Christendom. In fact, the church that I attend now is connected loosely with these people and their movement. I will go into more detail about this later. This and other encounters made me think that I needed to know more about what I really believed and to be able to speak with confidence about the things that I believed to be true.

The Bible talks about taking the first year of your marriage to stay home and "cheer" your new wife (Deut. 24:5). So, I took that to heart and was able to spend quite a bit of time with Suzanne getting to know her better. The job I had as a concrete truck driver paid more than the block factory job but the hours were not the same. I was only working half the hours but considering my circumstances, I felt it was okay. In fact, I was making similar money for half the time.

I learned that I could work on a master's degree through distance learning at Liberty University, so I started that not long after I got married. You were able to view the classes via video tape and take tests that had to be overseen by a proctor. I lived across the street from a Catholic seminary in Keego Harbor, so I talked to one of the sisters and she agreed to be my test proctor. I was attending a non-denominational church, studying at a Baptist Seminary, and had a Catholic test proctor! Again, this stirred up more mental confusion, yet I had a persistent intellectual desire to know the truth. I was seeking doctrinal truth and true Christian experience with God.

I was going to become a part of the Assembly of God denomination, but my plans changed one day when I was talking to people in Birmingham, near Bloomfield Hills, about their faith. I met a guy named Howard who was preaching in the park in the middle of the city. Our paths crossed one day and he invited me to hear a guy that he was associated with named "Holy Hubert" Lindsey. He said that Hubert was considered the father of the "Jesus movement" and was beaten blind, by the Hells Angels, in the Sixties for preaching on the Berkeley University campus during the Vietnam War protests and riots.

The country was in turmoil then, the Vietnam War was going and the students were protesting in mass numbers. I thought, I have to meet this guy. I heard him preach at a Church of God in nearby Rochester; he was very bold and took a strong stand against rock music and alcohol, which to me, at the time, seemed like a needed message. The pastor at that time seemed to be very upset and almost shut him down. After the service, he was not treated very well by the pastor, as I remember.

That was my first encounter with Holy Hubert. Later I learned that he was starting a church in Birmingham, a city that by the world's standards is rich both fiscally and intellectually. He was at 777 Bowers St., in an old garage that was owned by James Elisman, an attorney, who was helping Hubert financially and with a place to stay. Elisman had a house not far from the church and let Hubert stay there while he was working on starting the church. Hubert and Jim had a broadcast on a local radio station called "Churches on Trial." It was designed to challenge the churches in regards to doctrine and practice. Hubert was very bold–some would say brash–in his approach. He would call people out who would ask various questions and accuse them of being compromising in their behavior. He would warn people that if they continued in their ways that they would go to Hell.

Many non-believers called in and tried to make light of him and his message. Jim's famous line was "I cut him off, Hubert," meaning that Jim would hang up on the caller because he was acting belligerent. The program was on Sunday night, eleven p.m. to one in the morning. It was the most listened to show that WMUZ had at that time. He stirred up a lot of controversy as people disagreed with his radical stance against sin and some of his other positions including water baptism and sanctification. He would say that if you're a Christian you would not sin. You cannot sin and be a Christian, he would say. You can be a Christian and sin but you cannot sin and be a Christian. By this he meant that you can't practice sin and have no real change in your life and still claim to be a Christian.

He also had a strong view on water baptism, saying that it was not necessary for Christians to be water baptized because it was a work of the flesh that made people think that just because they were water baptized, that they were saved. How many people who were water baptized still live for the things of the world, thinking that just because they did this act, that it would secure them a place in God's Kingdom? He had some good points, and for sure, got everyone thinking and searching the Word for the truth about these issues. What I liked about him was his boldness and his unwavering stance against wrongdoing, which was something that I did not really hear very much since I had become a Christian. It seemed many preachers did not want to come out hard against sin, for fear of losing their congregations and bases of financial support.

I started going to the church Hubert was pastoring at night after I would attend Brightmore Assembly of God (AG) in the morning. I had talked to Thomas Trask the pastor at the AG church about getting credentials to become a minister. He was nice and helpful, and I felt that I was on the right track to become an ordained minister with the AG.

Hubert was looking for people to help him plant this church, and I recall one day he pleaded with us to help him start this work. I thought I needed to make a choice between getting credentials with the AG and helping him. Right or not, I chose to leave the AG church and help him start his work. Looking back, I wonder if I made the right decision.

Hubert had a way of persuading you and almost make you feel bad for him. If I did not believe that he was doctrinally sound and true, I would not have made this choice. I respected him highly for his faith and work and the suffering that he endured during his years as an evangelist. The church was small, but it was a close group and I really learned to love the members.

I started preaching in the park near the church, as many kids came out each week to talk and debate about the authenticity of the Bible and its statements about Hell for unbelievers. Things seemed to be going good; the church was growing, and I was having Bible studies in my apartment as well as preaching at the church, hoping to find a place of full time ministry. Hubert wanted to buy out old church buildings in Detroit and reach out to the communities from these places. So I felt that I was on the right track and through Hubert's ministry, I was also being greatly challenged in my thinking.

I did not just accept what Hubert said, but I studied it and all these years later am still studying it. Hubert actually preached with and knew Hagin and Copeland and the rest of the faith preachers. He would say they were "quite ignorant." He came out hard against the prosperity message and had some good points about healing and giving. He felt that many of the modern preachers were not well-read and doctrinally off. Like I said, I really respected him because he had a doctorate (at least that is what he said) and had preached with many of the popular guys and had suffered greatly for the cause of Christ.

At that time I really felt that the faith preachers that had never studied (most of them have no formal education or seminary degrees) or suffered for Christ were not reliable. In some ways I still do. Not all, but many, are so focused on success in this life that they miss the point. If they speak the truth in regards to the death, burial and resurrection I will say "amen," but when they fleece the flock for their own gain I part ways with them. I want to stay focused on the apprehension of truth and not personalities.

The reality is that most of the early church fathers differed on various points of doctrine yet many of them died for the faith. I used to be one hundred percent against the faith movement and its teachings, but now I judge individual teaching by its merit in light of what I know to be absolute truth. The truth is that God owns all and He does prosper people. The lie is that all must prosper in the same way according to the same method, in effect, if you say a certain prayer or give a certain amount you will get a certain thing. Jesus did not die to make us prosper. Prosperity was functional under the Old Testament; Jesus died to give us peace with God and secure us a place in heaven. If financial prosperity comes, thank God; if it doesn't come, thank God as well. Hebrews 11 is all about the faith of the fathers. Some prospered, some did not, but they were all commended because of their faith. More on that later.

The church did well for a couple years and then Hubert's health began to fail and because he did not appoint elders the church splintered into many pieces. I loved Hubert as much as I could love anyone, and though he spoke many things that were truth, I think that some of what he promoted was not in proper balance. Yet he helped me understand God's grace in a way that I did not understand it even though I was taught it many times.

The Gospel of God's grace is the central theme of the Bible. The Old Testament foretold the grace message, and the New Testament preaches it in its fullness. The Law came through Moses, but grace and truth through Jesus Christ (John 1:17). Though I had gone through Bible college and had much study of the Bible, I did not realize the fullness of the grace message. It really is grace that teaches us not only to deny worldly lust and live soberly in this age, but also it teaches us the great value of the cross (Titus 2:11-13). Not rules but grace.

The grace of God contains in it the desire and the ability to do what God says. It takes God to love God, it takes God to know God, and it takes God to serve God. None of us can do it on our own. Paul said, "it is God who is at work in you both to will and to do for His good purpose" (Phil. 2:12-13). Without the action of God in the human soul, it is all fruitless activity. John Piper wrote about grace in his book *Future Grace*. He writes, "...the grace of justification and the grace of sanctification are both by faith because faith is the one response to grace that guards the glory for God. Faith does not contaminate grace with human self-sufficiency. Therefore faith prevents boasting... Faith excludes boasting and exalts the glory of grace... we need to let it sink in that grace is not only gotten by faith, but glorified by faith...every moment of faith is a tribute to His Grace." It is the Lord who helps us and enables us to believe in an ongoing sense.

I actually wrote a senior paper about hearing the voice of God. The main theme of the paper was that, if you were in a place of being renewed in the spirit of your mind and transformed by the renewing of your mind, then you could hear the voice of God on a regular basis (Rom. 12:1-2). Living by the system of works will never make the heart sensitive to God. It takes us in one of two directions. You are either boasting about your activity or you're down because you have not done enough. Paul said, his only boast was the cross of Christ, nothing of his own but all of Him, and this is what compelled him to do what he did (Gal. 6:14). Isaiah said, "You will go out with joy and be led forth with peace. The mountain and the hills will break forth before you...." (Is. 55:12). The point is, when you really know you're accepted and truly loved, you enter rest, and from that rest you work, not to be accepted, but out of joyful desire. (Hebrews 4 is a great discourse on the true rest of God.) We are saved by grace through faith for good works which God has prepared beforehand that we should walk in them (Eph. 2:8-10). For good works, not to do them.

Chuck Colson wrote a book entitled *The Good Life* in which he tells about how God called him to prison ministry:

Did God declare His purpose for me during those first months after I was released from prison and was questioning what to do with my life? I had some very tempting offers in business and in law. I wanted to do something with my life that was far less public. I wanted to be with my kids and spend some time getting my life together. Yet I kept feeling a deep urge that I should be doing something for prisoners. That was not what I wanted to do. It's not a very glamorous way to spend your life. A Washington acquaintance who befriended me during this period and organized a small prayer group wanted me to work with political leaders through Bible studies. That would certainly have been logical. Still, I could not shake off the conviction that I should be in the prisons. Like Jacob of the Old Testament I wrestled with God until the break of day. Jacob ended up with a bad hip; I ended up with a conviction that I should be in the prisons. Was it Providence? It certainly was not my self-will.

This experience mirrors the many stories in the Bible that indicate a struggle that goes on inside as a result of the call of God for a particular direction: saved for good works which God has prepared (Eph. 2:10). Your call may not be as dramatic as that, but each day there is a call on your life to seek and find God and His will for your life.

Christianity is about *being*, not doing. Once the being is established (and only God knows when that is for each person), then the doing can occur. Many people are going to and fro seeking to establish their own work or ministry in God's name. Many are compelled with zeal, but it is not tempered with the right knowledge or the right timing. These things were becoming clearer to me, but I was still struggling both doctrinally and experientially.

I remember before I graduated from TFC, during spring break I purposed in my heart to go Florida to do some "beach preaching." After reading about John Wesley and George Whitfield, I was inspired to go outside of the "four walls" and into the streets to make Him known. At the time, whenever I was in church all I could think about was "souls." What are we doing here, I would think, when the multitudes are perishing?

George Wester, who was the original pastor of our church in Toccoa, had a cabin not far from the school located in a very remote place, the same one that Jeff and I went to. I decided to go to the cabin for a week to seek the Lord even though I felt guilty, like I should be preaching. Troubled by my lack of ability to hear God and feel that I was in His will, I went to the cabin. The first night I remember lying on a bench outside the cabin and telling the Lord to take my body as a sacrifice. I offered my body as a living sacrifice (Rom. 12:1-2).

That week I drank juice and water and prayed and read the Bible. Behind the cabin was nothing but woods, so on about the third day, I decided to go for a walk. I got totally lost. I was asking God to speak to me, night was falling and I was getting worried because I had no flashlight or matches and it was getting cold. I heard the inner voice say "go this way, turn that way." I really mean to tell you that I had no idea where I was yet, all of a sudden; I came to a gravel road and then got my bearings walked back to the cabin just before nightfall.

I thanked God for His direction. I thought, God really does speak and we can hear Him, but we have to listen with our spirits. I want to say here that, even though it is possible to hear God speak to our inner man, sometimes we may go through long periods for whatever reason when we do not hear clearly. Abraham heard God speak at strategic times. The Bible never gives the impression that God was speaking all the time, like, "Hey Abe, I want you to go down and feed the chickens today" or some such thing. God speaks, and I believe we can hear Him but that doesn't mean He will tell us what to wear or eat on a daily basis.

When I worked for the concrete company the trucks that we drove had radios in them. The radios were there for various reasons that related to the job, for answering questions like, where are you or how long is this particular job is going to take? One day, a driver flipped his truck and was asking for help. He was okay but, thankfully, he had a radio. The primary reason for the radio was to transmit information concerning the job, and in the same way, much of what God speaks to us in relation to the job He wants us to do. But in this case the radio was used to call for help. Sometimes we just need help and if we call God hears. After the crash I was in, my prayer life was reduced to couple of words: "help me." He cares about us, not just what we can do for Him. I used to think that God would only speak in relation to the ministry. But He will speak to us if we have "ears to hear" about everything. Psalm 16:11 says that "in His presence is fullness of joy and pleasures at His right hand forever." When we are in His presence we have joy and receive His help.

Abraham heard God's voice. When Abraham offered up his son in obedience to God, it was a great challenge. All his hopes and dreams, and even the promise of God, were in Isaac. Years earlier God had promised that through Abraham's seed all the nations of the earth would be blessed (Gen. 22:18, 26:4). He believed, and so it was credited to him as righteousness (Gen. 15:6). As time went by he became anxious about the promise of his seed blessing the nations and went into his handmaid Hagar after his wife suggested he do so (Gen. 16:2). There is no record of any argument on Abraham's part, but today we are still paying the price for this act of disobedience; "His hand will be against every man" (Gen. 16:11-12). The Muslim nations came out of Ishmael. They have been at war with Jews and Christians for centuries. The crusades and 9/11 and similar conflicts and attacks are motivated by the Koran when it says, "go and slay the infidels." The young men are promised young maids in heaven if they die for Allah. This is a prime way to motivate a young man and it works.

As the years went by, Abraham realized that if the promise was going to be fulfilled then it was going to have to be God doing it. His body was as good as dead, but still Abraham did not waver at the promise but grew strong in faith (Gen.17). Think about it; years earlier he was anxiously trying to fulfill the promise but now he was in a position where he was powerless to make it happen on his own.

God is into coming through when things are totally dead. Abraham had Sarah's dead womb. Moses had dead dreams. Jesus's body was dead. Paul talked about being dead to sin but alive to God (Rom. 6:1-6). God seems to come through when things are dead, and only He knows when they really are.

Perhaps you are totally discouraged and the promise that you felt God give you is not coming to pass. Abraham, in hoping against hope, believed and so became the father of many nations (Rom. 4:18). His faith was in God to fulfill His word and God did. Again, when things were totally dead on the human level, God came through. Think about it, God raised His dead Son. There is something about when things are dead. This is when, many times, He shows up. He knew Abraham was dead serious. It was no formula he was following to get something from God; it was just naked faith in the word of God and belief in what God said. As a result, through a miracle, Isaac was born.

As time went along, probably about twelve years or so, God says "it's time to give it up." Give up the son of the promise. There is no record of any argument. Abraham did what God said. Over the years he learned that it is safe to trust God and it is right to love Him, so he ascended the hill to give up his son (Gen. 22:1-19). This was the son of the promise. Isaac gave Abraham perfect joy as the promised son and as the son of his old age. Spiritually, this was the fulfillment of God's promise, that through Abraham's seed, all the nations of the earth would be blessed. When he saw Isaac he may have looked on him with delight, remembering how he tried to make it happen in his own wisdom and power and it didn't work. Now with Isaac all the waiting was now paying off.

He may have been a little delighted with his own faith when he heard God say, "Offer him up." Yikes, I'm sure human reasoning began to kick into high gear. "This can't be right, this is the promise, I can't kill the promise of God." He did not yield to these thoughts, though.

When I think of this story, I can't help but think of the many people that I've run into who would tell me, "God promised and God said and God told me so, now look, I'm being obedient and making it happen." This story comes to my mind and I think, have you died to this promise and is it in God's hands or are you doing this in your own power?

When Abraham raised the knife, being fully prepared to slay his own son, God said, "hold the show, I know you fear Me" (Gen. 22:2-19). Though this is a real story, I think it applies in a broader spiritual sense. When we receive a promise from God of what He will do for us or how he will use us, many times He will ask for it back. Offer your ministry up to God, your future, your hopes, ambitions, health, wealth, etc. Offer your body as a living sacrifice, not just your words. "These people honor me with their lips, but their hearts are far from me," Jesus said (Matt. 15:8-9). When we truly put it on the altar, we are freed from trying to make it happen–in the external in terms of doing and in the internal, what God is doing inside of us–and God is freed to be God in our lives and will be faithful to His Word, in His time. We can truly rest and be still and not fret and trust in God. Though I did not fully understand the fullness of this sacrifice of my own body, it was the beginning of what would be a series of sacrifices that God would have me make.

I think ministry is vital in our day. A good minister is a great treasure. However, it seems that the role of minister has been twisted into the role of entertainer or mini-god. There is much pressure on ministers to perform, and I sometimes wonder if many have had this true experience of offering their ministries up to God. This pressure has caused good men to fail morally and mentally. God doesn't need us; we need Him, and we need to be at rest with Him doing only what He has called us specially to do. Many times young men compare themselves with other ministers wanting what they have, but not understanding the price that has been paid for that call. We honor Abraham because of his faith, but we also see from his life that he was human and learned faith over time.

Chapter Seven

Dreams Adrift

The Church at Birmingham started to splinter, and Hubert's health began to fail, so many left and went elsewhere. I used to visit him in the nursing home right after he got sick and thought he was ready to die then. It turned out that he was to hang on for years, and he ended up in a nursing home in North Carolina. I found it amazing that all these people that supposedly loved him were nowhere to be found when he needed them. Maybe my reaction wasn't mature but this is how I felt at the time. When Hubert was stirring things up and was the "star of the show," everyone was all about him, but when he needed help they were nowhere to be found.

I think this type of thing is part of the territory for a true minister. Paul said, "All forsook me" (2 Tim. 4:16). In Hubert's case, though, it was found out that he was living, to some extent, a lie. It turned out that Hubert had been divorced and tried to cover it up. He later said that the Devil said that his ministry would be lost if he told the truth about it. I wondered why he would listen to the Devil after he went on and on about heeding the voice of God. He spoke strongly against divorce and made it seem like he had never been divorced. But the truth came out through someone that knew him at the church. Hubert's sister from Alabama came up to Michigan and confirmed the fact of his divorce. The story was that he came home one day and found his wife in bed with the sheriff. That was the end of the marriage. Only God knows the whole story.

I realized that it was time to go as well. I met a pastor from a Missionary Alliance church in Waterford, about ten miles north of Birmingham. He was looking for a youth pastor, and I was looking for a place for ministry. We talked, and it seemed like a perfect fit. The Missionary Alliance denomination is associated with the Bible college that I graduated from, so I thought that it would be a "God thing." I could get my credentials for ministry, some experience reaching out and building a youth group, and at the same time, I could build for any future that God would lead me to. Although I was going to go with the Assemblies of God, this door of opportunity opened, and it just seemed right. After I prayed about it, I agreed to take on the position. They would pay me one hundred-fifty dollars a week for twenty hours of service. I was still working at the concrete company and now was able to really be involved and prepare for the ministry.

We started the youth group out with three kids who were partially mentally disabled and a couple other young people who attended the church but had not been a part of the group because of the disabled kids. The pastor stressed that this was not a "maintenance ministry." This position was designed to reach out to the community, help build the kids' faith, and encourage them to be an active part of the church. Kids would reach their families, and God would draw parents into the church through the kids.

The experience I had had with kids and ministry up to that point was mostly of the street evangelism variety, like preaching in the open air, in parks and campuses and one-on-one, usually challenging them to believe. I spoke in schools and jails and was an associate pastor/youth pastor in Toccoa, but nothing as organized and structured as what the pastor wanted. I told him of my lack of experience, and he said he would help me, which he did at first. He also said that he would "go to bat for me" in relation to people or superintendents who might try to push me out and make it difficult for me. He said he was not treated right at his last church and was going to make sure it did not happen to me. I thought that since this was a denominational church, that as long as I was doing okay, I would not need to fear problems. I was just so eager to do the work, I had no idea that I would even need someone to "go to bat" for me. Slowly the group began to grow and kids from all sections of the surrounding communities were coming.

When we decided to attend this church, about four or five families followed us from Hubert's church and joined the church. One of the dads who came with us had a relationship with some young guys from his neighborhood that he was trying to bring to church. We were introduced to them (Shawn, Chip and Jason) and felt that we should welcome them to the group. These guys were city kids and rough around the edges, but I felt a love for them. I would pick them up in my S-10 pick-up truck for Sunday night church. At the meeting, we would do an activity for about twenty minutes, then worship for about twenty minutes, and then I would speak to them about twenty minutes.

Kids started coming from every direction, including those from financially stable homes and those who were not as fortunate. The group was growing. I was able to preach once a month in church on Sunday morning and was brought in as an official minister. I felt like I was finally moving in a direction. In fact, I was.

I was also still, on occasion, going to the campuses to preach in the open air, as I felt that this was always going to be a part of what I should do on a regular basis. On the campuses, we would cry out against all that is Biblically wrong, including homosexuality (Isaiah 58:1). A couple of other guys I'd met at Hubert's church and I were at the University of Michigan campus, and someone complained about our approach and called the pastor. He was "appalled" and took offense at us, not asking us about our position or what happened, but sided with the person, whom he had never met and who was probably just trying to defend her lifestyle (she was, in fact, a lesbian).

Throw a rock into a pack of dogs and the one that gets hit will bark the loudest. Outdoor preaching is a lot like that. Start preaching and the person who is most offended will yell and heckle the most.

Looking back, this was the beginning of the end of my time at the Missionary Alliance Church. The pastor seemed to cool toward us and many of the families that had followed us to the church, but the youth group kept growing and we continued to minister to the kids. I got a part-time job as a substitute teacher in Pontiac which gave me a greater connection to more of the kids, since many of them went to school in that district. The pastor was putting more pressure on me to keep a log of each thing I was doing every day to make sure I was putting in my required hours. I did it, though I felt that something was wrong.

Herb R. came to the church as a counselor fresh out of seminary. His wife had been raised in that church, and he set up an office in the church to do counseling and began to do the things that I did on Sunday morning, like preaching and giving announcements. Slowly I was being pushed out of my place. This was not just a feeling, but real. The pastor left on a vacation, and I was to preach that Sunday morning. Apparently, some took offense at the words and the way I was speaking. I admit that I was bold and a little loud, but I was not at all any louder or bolder than many others who preach. "TV Thomas," an evangelist, came to the church not long after that, and he was a lot louder than me. Some complained to the pastor and, though I had many who said they appreciated the message, the detractors seem to win out. When the pastor got back from vacation his attitude changed toward me, and though I meant no harm I could tell he had changed. The pastor called the district superintendent (D.S.) about me, and when I found out I was shocked. I called the D.S. and we set up a meeting. He was a nice man but we did not see eye-to-eye. I felt I had done no wrong, and that the ministry on the campus was Biblical and straightforward. Jesus preached about Hell and told people to repent and, as graciously as we could, that is what we were doing (John 7:7, Mark 1:15). He told me to read First and Second Timothy and call him in a few weeks.

The pastor told the elders that the church was changing direction, that it was going to focus on adult education, and that the youth group would no longer be necessary. I said I would continue as the youth pastor for no pay, but it was obvious that he wanted me out. I told him that I disagreed with him but would honor his decision as the pastor. Inside, I was dying. Not only was I wondering what I would do, I was concerned about the kids. I left the church and gave the elders a warning. I just felt like I had to tell them, " If you will not help the helpless and reach out to whomsoever will come, then this place will not last."

After I left, the families that followed us to the church left as well, and the pastor had a nervous breakdown. Later, after recovering from his break-down, he came back to the church and did a similar thing to Herb. He was upset that Herb was involved helping people who appeared demonized. I was at the elders' meeting when Herb said that one of the things he wanted to do was to help the demonized (people who were struggling with evil spirits). At that meeting all the elders were giving him the go ahead. They all seemed genuinely excited about what Herb wanted to do. For some reason, though, the pastor felt that he should move Herb out as well.

I was not at the meeting at the church when they "blew the whistle" on Herb, but I heard it was not good. Herb ended up leaving the church and the minister had another breakdown, and now the building is a school and the church is no more.

I say all this to say that leadership is vital. A bad leader can crush and ruin people and cause untold damage. My young friend Chip from the youth group died from a drug overdose, one of the girls that was so excited about God ended up pregnant, and many were broken and scattered. If you're ever a part of a situation similar to this, I want to encourage you to not give up your faith and to try to find a place in a healthy, well-balanced church. Only God knows what was going on in that pastor's mind. I will not even begin to speculate. I really felt like I was going to find a future there, but God had other plans. I wondered what I should do. At the time I was thinking about the health of my family and what was best for them. I knew I had a calling but realized that I needed to make sure my family was taken care of, for if I did not take care of them I was worse than an infidel (1 Tim. 5:8).

A further death to my dreams was taking place. I continued to try to find a place of ministry in a couple of churches, but felt that not only I, but my wife also, needed a place of healing and stability. We found a place that met the need and the pastor, who has spiritual gifts in teaching and prophesying, prophesied over my wife and I during one of the first services we went to. We felt blessed and assured that God was not done with us. Therefore, we attended Mount Zion church. At the same time, we were still in fellowship with some of the families from Hubert's and the Alliance churches and were meeting with them each week for Bible study. I thought things were going well, and the families we were with were hungry for God. I started to think that God wanted to take this to the next level.

I asked the people if they were game to start a church, and they all seemed excited about it. We asked to use the building of the father of one of our friends, who was a pastor, and he agreed to let us use the church in the afternoon. So, with about four families, we started. It seemed good at first, but gradually things started to fall apart. The wife of one of the brothers who was taking care of the money began to stray from her commitment to him. She ended up with another man. The men seemed to shift in their support for me and turned against me, in that they spoke about me in a wrong way and no longer were supportive. At that point, I told the rest of the people that they should consider going to Mt. Zion. I really felt that they needed what was being offered there. They refused to go, thinking that the church was not doctrinally sound, and they seemed offended that I would leave them. Many of them at that time had left the faith and their marriages were broken.

I feel broken over their souls, and I know if it were not for the grace of God, I would have left the faith. I went back to Mt. Zion and continued to preach on campuses. I felt that things were going well, except that I was not being used in the local church and was frustrated by that. I sensed a desire, right or wrong, to find my place, and even though the pastor had prophesied over me that I would be "a fruitful vessel in the house" and that I would "speak as an oracle of God," I was not seeing it and was anxious to make it happen. So, I left Mt. Zion and went on a search. I met with a man who was starting a church by my house. I told him a little of my story and that I wanted to get involved. At that point, I was really leery of pastors and was guarded in terms of my approach. No longer was I going just by my feelings and mere impressions, but I was questioning things more. I told the pastor that I would help him if he would help me. He told me that I could meet with some of the superintendents and start down the road of ordination. I thought long and hard about it and decided not to do it. One night, they had a group of preachers come and preach at the church, and they all sounded the same. I thought I could never fit in. I left the church feeling that this was not the place for me.

After I left that church, the pastor who said he was "there to stay" left the church and is now pastoring in a town forty miles south, under the title "Dr." He had not even been to Bible school. God is not impressed with your position or credentials. If you're reading this and you fit this description or are close, put the book down and repent, now. Many preachers use the people for their own satisfaction. A minister's satisfaction needs to be from his relationship with God, and he should be glad that he has the privilege of speaking life to the people of God. Give me a person who is satisfied to be a brother, called to give life to the people. I can't say I understand it all, but I do know that it is wrong to move in the flesh to accomplish the work of God. More brokenness was entering my heart as I left that place in search of a place where I could raise my kids in the fear and admonition of the Lord and, hopefully, be used by God. I began to be convicted that it was important to establish my kids in a place whether I was used or not.

I came full circle to the place I used to visit when I came up to visit my folks from college, Bloomfield Hills Christian Church, which had had some trouble back in the late 1980s, as the pastor had been caught in adultery. I was good friends with the current pastor's wife's brother, and decided to visit their new church. I talked to the pastor and he was anxious to get me started and made some promises that he would help me get started. At first, things seemed to be going well. I was preaching on Sunday nights and was a part of the home groups. I was able to meet and take out a number of young guys to the park and campuses to do some outdoor evangelism. Again some negative feedback was coming and yet, because the pastor was more understanding than others I had known, it was not a problem. I was just glad to be being used and my hope for future ministry was reviving.

Chapter Eight

Spiritual, Having a Human Experience

At the new church, I started coming up against the same type of frustrations I'd experienced at the other churches. The Sunday night service was cancelled, and every other possibility for preaching and teaching ministry in the church was cut off except for one, "The Master's Call Bible School." I have been at it since the school started in 1998, and it has proved to be a blessing. I have had much positive feedback. The call to teach and minister is partly becoming a reality, but the road has not been well-paved. In fact, when all these various losses and setbacks and misunderstandings were taking place in the outside world, my inside world was being tested and stripped to the very core. I'm still trying to put the pieces together, and I can't say I fully understand it, but I want to encourage you in your walk with

Him, to hold on when things are not going the way you feel they should be going. My friend told me, "adapt, improvise and overcome." The only reason I tell the story is to show that things happen that you do not understand in your walk of faith. You will be tempted to quit and give up your dreams; don't. Hold on because what God says will come to pass... it *will*.

I do not want to point fingers and blame people, because I believe in God's sovereignty and His control over all things, especially the church. I'm saying these things because so many people get hurt by us in the Body of Christ and leave. Many have been bruised beyond repair; if you have, I urge you to get back in the race and keep loving God's people. I know it's not the most glamorous thing to do, but it captures God's heart. It is evangelism; Jesus said, "by this shall all men know that you are my disciples: by the love you have one for the other" (John 13:35). Loving people, in many ways, is like a war, and in all phases of each battle it is not easy. When we are hurt or rejected, many times, it is very hard to rebound. We all want to feel "a part," to love and be loved.

In fact, at the moment as I write this, I'm sitting in my van at my son's hockey game. He is on the team, but is not suiting up because he is on the "reserved squad." I gave the coach the benefit of the doubt when he told me that Brad was not good enough, but when I saw the players that were playing ahead of him, I was convinced that he was being set aside for some other reason. I called the coach, but he is convinced that Brad is not good enough. I have played hockey all my life and have coached through the years, and I can say, from that standpoint, that he should not be sitting out. This is an example of how we can do everything, yet still not find a place. Many work hard, and yet still feel out of place. My heart was broken again and I say to God, I do not want my son to suffer the same rejection and scorn that I have suffered over the years. I tell him that quitters never win and winners never quit. He remains on the team, but is upset that he is not playing. Practicing without playing is hard, we all want to play, to go to the dance and not just dress up. I find it difficult to tell him about God's "great plan," when all my Christian life I have tried to follow it and had so many hard times.

That is the modern misunderstanding, that God loves you and has a wonderful plan for your life. This is usually understood to mean you will have a great job, a great family, with health and wealth to spare. However, your life is your life. What you do or have is only a part of your life, but Zoë life is spirit life, and your life is your spirit. The God-man, Christ Jesus, was despised and rejected of men. It pleased the Lord to bruise Him (Is. 53:3,10). The Father looked down on the Son's humiliation and was pleased. Yet, Jesus had perfect peace. Contrast this with the thinking of being accepted only if you perform in a certain way or accomplish a certain thing.

The idea that you're going to have it all in this life, if you're a Christian is in error. I believe in remaining positive and hopeful for better days, but to say that you will avoid all suffering and you will have unlimited health and wealth if you love God is just not true. No doubt God will bless us with many great things, for which we are grateful, but to really have the power to enjoy them is another thing. How many have "everything" but are not happy?

Many of God's people have suffered greatly in their lives and for the cause of Christ. Jesus died on a cross, Paul was martyred under Nero (says Christian history), and James was killed by Herod (Acts 12:1,2). John the Baptist got his head chopped off (Matt.14:10,11), and John the Beloved was boiled in oil on the island of Patmos, according to church tradition. Moses spent forty years tending sheep when the call of God was on his life to deliver the children of Israel (Exodus 3:1). David was trained under a demonic king when he was anointed by the prophet Samuel to be King of Israel. He ran for his life and suffered many setbacks, some because of his own wrong choices (1 and 2 Samuel). Job, a man of faith, whom God called upright and blameless (Job 1:8), was put to the test, losing his family and his health for many years. He did not sin with his mouth, and in the end the Lord restored his losses (Job 1:22,2:10,42:12).

God wants to bless his people. He has no trouble in doing it, but He looks for His image in us (Rom 8:28-30). To be conformed to His image, many times He uses the fire of testing. No one wants to be put to the test and suffer to be conformed to His image, but this is many times, though not always, the pathway. If you ask a young person what they want to be when they grow up they will usually say a doctor, lawyer, or some other occupation. None will stand up and say "I want to be made more like Christ through suffering." That is just not in their thought process at all.

Jesus learned obedience through the things that He suffered (Heb. 5:7-8). Are we greater than He? Because of Adam's sin the world is fallen, it is decaying. The second law of thermodynamics states that things are winding down, that they are decaying. All material changes over time. It has a half-life, and turns into something else. (Just look in the mirror!) When things die, they change and decay into dust. God made our bodies out of dust, and when we die our bodies will go back to the dust. He breathed into Adam the breath of life, and Adam became a living soul (Gen. 2:7). The soul is the breath of God, but as a result of the Fall, our beings were contaminated with wrong thoughts and intentions (Rom. 5:12). Thus began the dying process.

God is pro-life, but death was our choice in the beginning. God commanded Adam not to eat of the tree of the knowledge of good and evil, and warned, "In the day that you shall eat thereof in that day you shall surly die" (Gen. 2:16-17). Sin came into the world through one man, Adam, and death by sin and sin was passed on to all men because all have sinned (Rom. 5:12). All have sinned and fallen short of the glory of God (Rom. 3:23). Death in the Greek, means not the elimination of life or annihilation, but rather separation. According to Vine's *Dictionary of New Testament Words* the word *phantanos* means "separation of the soul (the spiritual part of man) from the body (the material part of man), the latter ceasing to function and turning to dust, e.g., John 11:13, Hebrews

:7, 7:23... the separation of man from God; Adam died on the day that he disobeyed God, Gen. 2:17... death is the opposite of life; it never denotes nonexistence, as spiritual life is 'conscious existence and communion with God, so spiritual death is conscious existence and separation from God." Adam could still walk and talk, but things were not the same. A sense of shame and loss filled his life, and he knew he was naked. In the beginning, Adam and Eve were naked and unashamed, but now, after their sin, they were covered with shame (Gen.2:25,3:7).

A psychology that does not understand this concept will never truly help the person, for it will only be dealing with symptoms and behavior, but never the root cause. No doubt we are complex creatures, but recognizing the Lord's purpose in the great picture is very important. Jesus deals with the heart, the inner man. He resides in the heart of the believer, and Paul prays for the Christians at Ephesus to be made strong in the inner man (Eph. 3:16). This has everything to do with you and your disposition. Activity and work are good things and honorable, but Jesus came to die for you not your work. We really are primarily spiritual having a human experience, not the other way around.

So there is God's sovereign will and His protection over His people, and there is sin operating in the world along with God's gift to the human family, free will. This is what our minds can't fully grasp, and this is where we must exercise faith. Many today feel that God will protect us from all harm. I want to show from Scripture that this is not so.

Charles Haddon Spurgeon said, "the old covenant was a covenant of prosperity and the new a covenant of adversity." What does this really mean? Deuteronomy 28 talks about being blessed "in the field and the basket, and the fruit of your womb, and your storehouses," opening the heavens and basically commanding a blessing on all of your external life. You would be the head and not the tail, above and not beneath (Deut. 28:1-14). If you obeyed, you would be blessed and if you disobeyed, you would suffer a curse (Deut. 28:15-68). This is a covenant that was given to Israel to show forth the goodness and power of God to the surrounding nations. God was showcasing His people to the nations, and the outward prosperity was the evidence that He was who He said He was.

There is disagreement among scholars on this point, but it is right here that many of the problems and disagreements lie. Many stand on this passage and really have built their empires based on these verses and other verses that support it. "Follow God and be healthy and wealthy. Obey and be blessed, disobey and be cursed, it's as simple as that." The logic, then, is when someone is sick or not well, they must be disobedient. After all, the logic goes, Psalm 91 states that "Surely He shall deliver you from the snare of the fowler and from the perilous pestilence." You should never suffer from any harm, or at least extreme harm, according to these verses, unless, of course, you are not obedient. When you really think about it, it is a very cruel system based entirely on performance, but this was an old contract. (By the way, not one person, with the exception of Jesus ever obeyed the whole law.)

A new contract is always better, and this new contract is based on an inward work in the heart that has nothing to do with outward material items or physical heath. Hebrews 8:7-13 talks about this new covenant: "For this is the covenant that I will make with the house of Israel after those days says the Lord: I will put My Laws in their minds and write them on the their hearts; and I will be their God and they shall be my people." Writing the Law on the heart and mind is different than blessing you with all outward things (Heb. 8:10). Jesus said, "be on the alert against all kinds of greed because a man's life does not consist in the abundance of his possessions" (Luke 12:15).

Notice he did not say "obey and be blessed," like it said in Deuteronomy, but rather the opposite. Jesus was not preaching the Law; He was bringing a new thing. The prophet said, "behold I do a new thing and before it happens I will announce it" (Is. 43:19). The prophets foretold that Jesus was coming, and John the Baptist announced it. The Kingdom is at hand. The King is here and it is a new day. The requirement of this Kingdom was of the heart not just of works. The Law said, "Do and you will have." The grace package said, "Repent and live."

Jesus called people to follow him whatever the cost. "Foxes have holes and birds have nests, but the Son of Man has no place to rest His head" (Matt. 8:20). He told the rich man to sell it all and follow Him (Matt. 19:21). Christ was God in flesh and He did not say, as under the Law, "if you obey you will be blessed in the field and basket, etc." He said you obey by believing (John 6:29, 3:36, 5:24). Obedience has to do with faith and trust in who He is and what He has done for us on the cross, and what the Holy Spirit does on the inside of a person. Believing is obeying, and when you truly believe you will obey. You will "walk by the Spirit and you will not fulfill the lusts of the flesh" (Gal. 5:16). God's work is an inward work that enables us to actually be who we are supposed to be, to be free to love God, whether we have little or much or whether we are healthy or not.

In America things are, at the time of this writing, favorable to Christians and the economy is decent. There are principles that, if followed, will help your outward life in terms of increased possessions, such as hard work, being generous and giving to God your first fruits (Prov 3:9-10). We need to trust God in the area of finances and be good stewards of all that He allows us to have. You may prosper (which some think is to be made rich) or you may not, outwardly, in terms of money, but always you can have peace inside (not on the basis of how much you have or how well you are doing physically).

A casual reading of Paul demonstrates the absurdity of the idea of unlimited external prosperity as the result of obedience. He was a Jew, a Pharisee and a keeper of the Law (Phil. 3:4-6). If anyone should have prospered outwardly, it would have been him. On the contrary, he talks about his trials, setbacks and troubles (2 Cor. 4:7-12, 2 Tim. 4:6-15). His life confirms what Spurgeon says about this New Covenant. It is one of adversity as a result of preaching the Gospel. Paul was obedient and thus had power to tell the world the truth (Acts 1:7-8).

This New Testament gives you an inner freedom that is based on the assurance of eternal life and that no matter what happens you will be able to say, "God loves me and He is with me" (Heb. 13:5-6). The first commandment is to love the Lord your God with all that you are (Ex. 20:3, Matt. 22:37-38). How can this be possible if something doesn't take place inside to produce this? Most people can perform a task or follow an order and get certain results. Do "A" and get "B;" it works. But when it does not work, then what?

Again, the Law or Old Covenant focuses on doing, while the new on the heart or inner man. Under this new agreement, you may suffer great loss outwardly like the Hebrews who joyfully accepted the plundering of their property, because they saw something else other than this world (Heb. 10:32-39). Those who live godly lives will suffer persecution (2 Tim. 3:12). In these passages, we see that this new agreement does not promise us a rose garden, but rather trials and troubles in the battle to get the word out. And in this battle we are made more like Jesus and are drawn closer to Him.

As I lived in relation to the Charismatic side of Christian experience, I have noticed that the mixing of covenants is very common. Deuteronomy 28:1-14 is often quoted and stood behind to give the impression that, if I obey God I will be blessed like Israel was promised in the Old Testament. Little mention is given to the adversity side of things, and much is made of the prosperity side. When there is confusion on this point the word cannot be rightly divided. Truth not rightly divided in the pulpit will bring bondage in the pew. Even though this theology sounds good, in many cases its focus is wrong and many end up with a lottery mentality, hoping for the "return on their seed," like buying a lottery ticket hoping to win. People who are not physically and financially well struggle, feeling there is something wrong with them if they are not seeing money coming back to them as the result of their offerings or are struggling with being sick. I have struggled much with this whole concept through the years and have tried to find the truth in doctrine and experience. On one hand I could see the truth of prosperity and healing, but on the other side I struggled with how it was presented.

Hank Hanegraaff is a well-known apologist and radio personality who took the place of Walter Martin. Martin wrote the *Kingdom of the Cults*, and Hanegraaff took his place on his radio program that focused on the "defense of the faith." One day I heard him talking about the faith movement. His arguments were so persuasive that it made me think about the church I was attending. They have strong "word of faith" leanings, and now, as with Dave Hunt T.A. McMahon in the past, the same thing was happening again in my thinking. I would listen to the "Bible Answer Man" program on my way home from work and, I have to tell you, he made a lot of sense. I got his book *Christianity in Crisis* and the tape series that went along with it. He took actual quotes from guys like Kenneth Copeland and Kenneth Hagin. After reading Hanegraaff, I have to say some of what is taught by these men is questionable. Listen to what they say if you want, and "eat the meat but spit out the bones." Hanegraaff will say they are false teachers and not consider them Christians at all. Educated and Godly people would disagree with him. I reject any erroneous teachings and will counter them when I have opportunity. As I said about the covenants, many of these men mix them, making us think that the more we have the more God likes us.

At the time though, Hanegraaff was truly challenging my thinking, and I wondered if I should leave the church that I was attending. I was reasoning that if the church was associated with the "faith people" at all, then I should leave. However, I did not hear erroneous teaching coming from the pulpit. The people who attended the church were good people, and the pastor wanted me to come and be a part and said he would help me get started in ministry. The word coming from the pulpit seemed balanced, and I detected no heresy. As in times past, when I was pondering Dave Hunt's writings, I was forced to rethink my theology. It takes time to determine what is really true, but the pursuit of truth is a noble one. Some people seem to be able to just accept the Bible as truth and not question it. It is simple child-like faith that is commendable. Some need more, though, and this is also commendable. I really believe that God wants us to be equipped to know and defend what we believe. To be able to give an account of the hope that is in us (1 Peter 3:15). This demands study and research.

Again, the only reason I'm telling this story is because I think that many people go through this type of struggle at one level or another and leave churches and ministries or get off on their own or leave the faith altogether. I have seen it through the years. Hank Hanegraaff and Dave Hunt made me think through my theology and stretched my thinking. I think that in many ways they are accurate, but as with all men, they are limited and mainly provide a springboard for further thinking. Kenneth Copeland and Kenneth Hagin and the many other word of faith personalities also stretch my thinking. They are not intellectuals but simple in their approach and seem to be well-meaning. They challenge people to believe God for all things. They may go overboard in some ways, and I disagree with some of their views but, as with Hunt and Hanegraaff, they provide a way to go deeper and think in a broader way.

I know many will disagree and think I am being double-minded. I used to think I had to choose sides. It was one group or the other. But now I just try to learn from each person. I don't agree with many Catholic views, but many Catholics live godly lives and believe in the triune God. God will separate the wheat from the chaff in the end (Matt.13:24-30). The most important thing is to think through our own theology and not be afraid of what others think but try to be sound in what we believe and move forward with God. Enoch walked with God and was no more (Heb. 11:5). Notice he walked "with God," not theology or what people said. He simply walked with God. What does the Lord require but to do justly and to love mercy and walk humbly with God (Micah 6:8). When all is said and done that is what we should do. That's it.

I believe in traditional Christian theology but that does not cause me to know God intimately. *Gnosko* in the Greek means "knowledge by experience," and this is what brings the soul into communion with Him. Many know theology and have right thinking but have no experience (like the Pharisees and Sadducees and the chief Priests and scribes in Jesus' times). And vice versa. John Piper writes in his book *Future Grace*, "When you believe merely on the basis of a testimony (the written word) you might assent to truth without delighting in it or seeing it as spiritually beautiful. But when you believe because you have had a spiritual taste or apprehension of spiritual beauty, the faith itself is permeated by this taste of spiritual beauty." He goes on, "...we may believe on the testimony of those in whose veracity and judgment we confide, that a man of whom we know nothing has great moral excellence. But if we see for ourselves the exhibition of His excellence, we believe for other reasons, and in a different way." It has taken me years to just begin to come into some soundness, and I'm continuing to grow. (I've always felt God and the soundness of His Spirit and the sound mind that He gives but in relation to my theology it has been a mental exercise.) I only hope that you, by reading this, will be helped in your thinking and your experience. For the last few years, some of this has come into clearer focus and now, since the crash which left me paralyzed in 2002, I have been faced with deep struggles that have caused me to think even deeper still. Life can cause you to go deeper or give up, to get bitter or become better.

Here is another example of what I'm talking about in relation to faith and prosperity. What you have or don't have is not evidence of your faith of lack thereof. The real issue is whether you still have faith even though things are not going right. Believing that things should always prosper and then when they don't can be like relying on a car that does not work. What good is the car if it doesn't work? What good is God if He doesn't work, one may conclude? The heart screams out in suffering, "this is not fair and God you don't work! If you did work, I would not be in this position! One may even point to the covenant that says I would be blessed and have no problems, and conclude, what's this?"

It's quite amazing, when God brought His people out of bondage they were given manna to eat. Manna actually means "what's this?" (Ex. 15:16). They were taken out of great bondage and slavery, but in their bondage they had lots of good things to eat, like leeks, onions, and meat (Ex. 16:3). When in the desert with God, they thought about the stuff they used to have and forgot the slavery part. When things got hard, they wanted to go back to Egypt to the security of bondage. "What's this?" We want our appetites filled with good things. Yeah we were slaves, but we don't like this manna. It's amazing how people act when what they love is taken away, even if they get something better.

131

Freedom from Pharaoh was forgotten, only what was lost was remembered. This is human nature; we all want to recapture the "glory years," and if we have to sacrifice spiritual freedom to get there, so be it.

I know men who have left decent marriages, not perfect, for something "better." When the pressure gets great in any sphere of life, the natural response is to want to get out. If we fall into a hole, we immediately try to find ways to get out. In the desert, God's people wanted to go back to Egypt. When the fire gets hot in the church people want out. I heard recently that twenty million people that were once church goers are now not going to any church. People are hurt and, instead of reconciling, they leave and never come back. It really is an epidemic. When Moses led God's people out it was first to the desert to worship and then to the Promised Land. When life is hard, and you're in a desert, it is preparation for the Promised Land.

You may achieve your dreams and enter into the fullness of your Promised Land, which means a feeling of knowing you are in God's perfect will, or you may die without your personal dream fulfilled. The dream of the Old Testament prophets was to see the Messiah, and they died without seeing Him; in the same way we may not see the fullness of what we hope for, but if we love God we shall find a place in eternity (Heb.11:39). This life is a preparation for an eternal kingdom and the ultimate Promised Land. Paul said, "For I consider that the sufferings of this present time are not worthy to be compared with the glory which shall be revealed in us" (Rom. 8:18).

Before my crash on April 26, 2002, I taught apologetics (defending the faith) at the Master's Call Bible School, and we were able to discuss the issues that skeptics and atheists raise concerning suffering and other hot topics. I have always felt bad for people in wheelchairs and would pray for them. In fact, there was a man in our church that is in a wheelchair who I prayed for not long before my accident. I would feel bad for him, thinking he was feeling condemned by the messages that were coming forth about healing and health. I really wanted to see him healed, and I hoped he would not be discouraged by the message of total healing and prosperity.

As I have already said, the Bible does say many things about being blessed in every way. "Every good and perfect gift comes down from the Father of lights" (James 1:16-17). "He who gave His own Son how much more will He give us all things?" (Rom. 8:32). Many verses focus on these types of things, but if you're not careful, you can see only one side of the coin. You can view Niagara Falls from many different angles. We can view God and suffering from many angles.

It is said that perception is reality, but what is the truth? Things are not the way they appear many times, and there is an unseen world. The Bible says that the Devil "prowls about like a roaring lion, seeking whom he may devour" (1 Peter 5:8-9). This means that there is a natural world as we know it with our senses, and a spiritual world that we believe by faith but may or may not have a great deal of understanding of. Many times people stare at one dimension of God and skip the rest. For example, seeing how Jesus healed people while He was on the earth. If he healed people on the earth and He is not changed then He will heal people today. This is one view, but again, it is only one view, and in God's overall plan it may be a very limited and shallow view. It is true that He healed and is the same yesterday today and forever, but it is also true that He is in total control and will be faithful to His worldwide plan, which may or may not include healing to all. Should people believe God for healing? Yes. Should they feel condemned if it doesn't come right away? No.

As I taught and we discussed these things, it became more and more clear that if we have hope for this life only we are, of all men, the most to be pitied (1 Cor. 15:19). I just got done reading a book by Don Piper, titled *90 Minutes in Heaven*. I encourage you to read it. It is a true story about Don, a Baptist preacher, who was hit by a semi-truck on a bridge and was pronounced dead. For ninety minutes, he was in Heaven and saw and heard remarkable things. His friend prayed him back, and he began the arduous recovery process that has lasted years. He longs to be in Heaven and looks forward to it and has been able to encourage many who are suffering with a reminder that Heaven is real. Even when there are no real answers or "good" that we can see in this life, it doesn't matter, God is still God. Jesus said about Himself, "blessed are those who do not see yet still believe" (John 20:29). Seeing and believing are two different things. If we have sight then we no longer need faith.

Suffering. Really, what is it? When I think of it, I think of things not being right, not normal, and out of whack, like a car that is not running properly. I think that for most people they would think that way. The Random House *Unabridged Dictionary* defines "suffer" as "to undergo or feel pain or distress, to sustain injury, disadvantage or loss, to undergo a penalty as of death, to undergo or experience (any action, process or condition): to suffer change." Where I live, there is a town that is one of the richest in the country and right next to it one of the poorest cities in the country. Great prosperity and great poverty. For most people, if they have a roof over their head and food in the refrigerator and a decent job to pay the bills, then there is a sense of normalcy. Some like a nicer home, others do not care if they live in an older home or not-so-nice place. We look at the homeless and say that is not normal. People starving or living in hard conditions, by our estimation, is not normal. There are many forms of suffering, to be sure. But for our definition let's say that suffering is out of the ordinary.

In our human condition, we focus on our health and wealth and the power to enjoy them. If we have these things then for the most part we can say that we are not really suffering. If you have health or wealth and it is taken away you are suffering, maybe worse than someone who has never known health or wealth. In America and many developed nations there has been a shift in the economic structures. Consider the following by Ralph Winter in his book *The World is Flat*:

America today is a save-yourself society if there ever was one. But does it really work? The underdeveloped societies suffer from one set of diseases: tuberculosis, malnutrition, pneumonia, parasites, typhoid, cholera, typhus, etc. Affluent America has virtually invented a whole new set of diseases: obesity, arteriosclerosis, heart disease, strokes, lung cancer, venereal disease, cirrhosis of the liver, drug addiction, alcoholism, divorce, battered children, suicide, murder. Take your choice. Labor-saving machines have turned out to be body-killing devices. Our affluence has allowed both mobility and isolation of the nuclear family, and as a result, our divorce courts, our prisons and our mental institutions are flooded. In saving ourselves we have nearly lost ourselves.

The point is well taken; suffering is universal in all generations. The wealthy suffer and the poor suffer. Some seem to avoid a lot of it, but sooner or later, everyone will die, and even if you die in your sleep peacefully after living a long healthy life, the thought of death has an enslaving power that most people cannot avoid (Heb. 2:15). The fear of meeting God and not being right. This is a dreadful condition.

Job in the Bible was an upright man who had a great family, wealth and health. "There was a man in the land of Uz whose name was Job; and that man was blameless and upright, and one who feared God and shunned evil and seven sons and three daughters were born to him. Also, his possessions were seven thousand sheep, three thousand camels, five hundred yoke of oxen, five hundred female donkeys and a very large household, so that this man was the greatest of all the people of the East" (Job 1:1-3). The common-sense reading of this passage is that Job is a God-fearing/loving blameless man who was rich with goods and family. "Now there was a day when the sons of God came to present themselves before the Lord, and Satan also came among them. And the Lord said to Satan, 'From where do you come?' So Satan answered the Lord and said, 'From going to and fro on the earth and from walking back and forth on it'"(Job 1:7). Satan is pictured walking on the earth, and he appears when sons of God come to honor the Lord. Now it is important to note here that Satan is real and he has access to the earth but it is God who begins a conversation with Satan. "Then the Lord said to Satan, have you considered my servant Job, that there is none like him on the earth, a blameless and upright man, one who fears God and shuns evil?" (Job 1:8). Without this background the book of Job can be made to say many different things that the theme of the book is not saying.

As you continue to read the first two chapters you get this dramatic picture of a behind-the-scenes look at what is going on in heaven while one is having problems on the earth. The Devil actually accuses Job before God that Job loves God because God protects and blesses him. "Have you not made a hedge around him, around his household, and around all that he has on every side? You have blessed the work of his hands and his possessions have increased in the land. But now, stretch out Your hand and touch all that he has, and he will surely curse You to Your face" (Job 1:10-11). God made Job to prosper and Satan's accusation is that if God takes it away, then Job will reject God. The Lord allows Satan to take his family (Job 1:13-19) and then his health (Job 2:7-8). After all this tragedy hits him, his wife tells him, "Do you still hold fast your integrity? Curse God and die!" (Job 2:9). Imagine, after losing your family and then being stricken with boils all over your skin, having your wife mock you and insult your faith. "In all this Job did not sin with his lips" (Job 2:10). His friends heard about him and came to comfort him. They were so grieved that they sat down with him for seven days and nights speaking nothing to him (Job 2:11-13).

This background is so important to interpreting the rest of the book. If we don't establish these facts that, by God's estimation, Job was upright and that Satan was allowed to afflict Job, then the book will not make as much sense. God has permitted this book in the Bible for our benefit so that when tough times come we will not be drowned in despair. The next chapters, from three to thirty-eight, are a dialogue between Job and his friends. Back and forth they went about God and what he was doing and why. In Chapter Three, Job is suicidal, "May the day perish on which I was born, and the night in which it was said a male child is conceived (Job 3:1). He goes on for the rest of Chapter Three complaining about his life. Probably the best thing for his friends to do would have been to stay quiet and just mourn for this man but they don't.

What they said came out of what they believed about who God was. "Then Eliphaz the Temanite answered and said, 'If one attempts a word with you will you become weary, but who can withhold himself from speaking" (Job 4:1-2). "... But as for me, I would seek God. And to God I would commit my cause" (Job 5:8-27). He goes on to talk about how God works and that, if Job would believe, then God would bless. "For you shall have a covenant with the stones of the field, and the beasts of the field shall be at peace with you. You shall know that your tent is in peace; you shall visit your dwelling and find nothing amiss" (Job 5:23-24). In other words "come on Job, have faith and God will bless you." Job's response was more grief, "Oh, that I might have my request, that God would grant me the thing that I long for! That it would please God to crush me, that He would loose His hand and cut me off!" (Job 6:8). Eliphaz' words actually brought more despair to Job. He goes on until Chapter Eight groaning and defending himself. His next friend, Bildad the Shuhite, said, "If you would earnestly seek God and make your supplication to the Almighty, if you were pure and upright [remember that God in the beginning said he was blameless and upright] surely he would awake for you and prosper your rightful dwelling place. Though your beginning was small your latter end would increase abundantly" (Job 8:5-7). It really sounds good and yet as we will see it is limited in scope. Job complains until Chapter Eleven. Then Zophar the Naamathite answered, "If you would prepare your heart and stretch out your hands toward Him, if iniquity were in your hand and you put it far away and would not let wickedness dwell in your tents, then surely your could lift up you face without spot; yes, you could be steadfast and not fear" (Job 11:13-15). The assumption from these men is that Job is not upright and needs to get things right and if he does then things will change.

We say the same thing to people, "turn to God and be at rest and God will begin to bless you." We, almost without thinking assume that if a person really turns to God that He will make it all better. In fact we may ask what is wrong with what Job's friends are saying? Unless you read the rest of the book and read where God rebukes these men, "And so it was after the Lord had spoken these words to Job, that the Lord said to Eliphaz the Temanite, 'My wrath is aroused against you and your two friends for you have not spoken of Me what is right, as my servant Job has'" (Job 42:7). After God speaks to Job directly in Job 38-41 He settles the issue with Job, "Now prepare yourself like a man..." he tells Job (Job 40:7). Job comes to the conclusion that God is God and He does things according to His will. "I know that You can do everything and that no purpose of Yours can be withheld from You" (Job 42:2). He then says, "I have heard of You by the hearing of the ear, but now my eye sees You. Therefore, I abhor myself and repent in dust and ashes" (Job 42:5-6). Job got a new understanding of who God was and, like Isaiah who saw the Lord and said, "I am undone," in the same sense Job's heart was broken. He saw that deep

inside he didn't know it all and God wa
than he was. No longer was it about defen...
was about seeing the fact that God really is and ...
purposes are *His purposes* and we are, at best, sinful
beings in need of God and His mercy and grace. Job
prayed for his "friends" and the Lord blessed him.
"And the Lord restored Job's losses when he prayed
for his friends" (Job 42:10). Indeed the Lord gave Job
twice as much as he had before. In Job's life he ended
up more blessed in the end than in the beginning.

When we look around at ourselves and others
we are tempted to make judgements that are made
to soon and in the end they are not right. Many times
we condemn ourselves and others to soon and thus
live in a state of never being at rest. Job was really
frustrated by his "friends" but after he really heard
God and God set things straight inside him, he was
able to pray for his friends. Many times we focus
on the person who caused us harm. In my case, the
woman who injured me while driving drunk. In your
case, it is someone else who hurt you or your family.
Like Job, we all need to let God speak and when He
speaks we obey and rest in His purposes even though
we don't understand everything that is going on.
Forgive, give and live. Job's forgiving of his friends
came out of his closer walk with God. Jesus said,
"Bless those who curse you and pray for those who
spitefully use you" (Matt. 5:44). Whatever has come
to you has come by God's providence, how you deal
with it will determine where you end up.

The Laodicean church said, "We are rich and
increased with goods and have need of nothing"

(Rev 3:17). I think the last statement was what God was really angry about. "You have need of nothing? Really?" They had lost their dependence on God. They were not desperate for Him. They were self-sufficient. Sometimes when "all is well," we are unaware of the plight of many people, and we are also tempted to not trust God for all things. Let me say it again, your lack of material goods and your poor health has nothing to do with your faith. If you are rich or poor, you must still lean hard on Him daily. In fact, if you're well off financially, you may have more temptations than the man who is struggling to survive each day.

We all have a tremendous thirst for God that will never be quenched; even in Heaven we will be craving more of God. Sadly, much of the hunger and thirst for righteousness is drowned by all that the world has to offer. Jesus said the Word is choked by the cares, worries and pleasures of this world (Mark 4:18-20). Larry Crabb wrote a book called *Shattered Dreams*. The main theme of the book is that God will allow certain dreams to shatter in order to draw us closer to Him and His dream for us. He writes:

> Our search for God is therefore an inward search. Silence and solitude are essential to discovering His Presence. We must block out the noise of life and become aware of our interior world if we're to find God. Beneath every heartache, beneath every moral failure, beneath every shattered dream, a divine Presence is waiting to be discovered. Why then do so few find

Him? Because He is hidden. Like a city after an earthquake, God's Presence is hidden beneath the rubble of the Fall. Look inside. An honest look will first reveal the rubble of our efforts to make life work without God, of our terror that keeps us from naked vulnerability to anyone, of our construction project that has created a false self that we hope will stay together through life. This is the rubble of dust and stone that hides the Presence. We live in sheer dread of giving up control and abandoning ourselves to God. Only when we discover a desire for Him that is stronger than our desires for relief from pain will we pay the price necessary to find Him. If we're to encounter the divine Presence we must enter the interior sanctuary of our heart and, like Jesus in the temple become indignant over what we find. There is no way to God but through the rubble. We must go through, not around, whatever keeps us from Him. The process is what spiritual people call brokenness and repentance.

Paul planted many churches and saw and performed many miracles, and yet, at the end of his life, he is in a prison. Not the kind of prison that we have in America but a shack with chains and a dirt floor. Each day he would have to make a determination that he was going to seek God. Much is made of the miracles in the book of Acts, but little is made of the seeming lack of deliverance of great men of God through the years. It was in prison where Paul wrote much of the New Testament.

Again, stressing only one side of the story can lead to frustration when we don't see instant deliverance. We need to keep believing but also to recognize that it is God who is at work in us, both to will and to do for His good purpose (Phil. 2:13). Crabb goes on to say, "That does not mean, of course, that we should dwell every minute on what is difficult in our lives. We would get nothing done and be good to no one if we did. More often, we should lighten up, enjoy what's enjoyable, and seize everyday opportunities to trust God and do well." I want to urge you in your struggle to begin to move in the direction of truly trusting God and asking for His direction each day and truly believe that he will "direct your paths" (Prov. 3:5,6). Notice "paths" is in the plural. We all have many paths and responsibilities, and we have to develop the belief that God is directing each road that we are on.

Chapter Nine

The Crash

Up to this point I have had my share of suffering in terms of my ministry career. Now something else was going to be attacked. My health. On April 26th, 2002 I was driving home from work at about 6:00 p.m. My wife called and asked if I would stop at the store and get some sauce for stir fry. I think I can manage that, I thought, so I stopped, got the sauce and got back in my two-door Blazer and put my seat belt on. I resumed heading north on Baldwin Road. About two miles north of the store, there is a crossroad called Clarkston Road, and just past the intersection at Clarkston Road it begins to wind in an "S" shape. I did not know that earlier that day a thirty-eight year-old woman who lived nearby had been drinking–all day. The story is that her boyfriend killed himself in front of her and her two children a year earlier and this is how she was dealing with her "pain," by becoming completely intoxicated (I don't know whether the boyfriend's suicide story is true or not but from what I know of her I tend to believe it) .

She did not stop with just becoming drunk but got in her car with her two kids and two of the neighbor's kids. I do not know where she was going, but she was heading south on Baldwin Road. When she got to the curves she crossed the double line into my lane and her low-to-the ground Saturn got under my Blazer which was higher off the ground. This resulted in the Blazer being flipped into a roll-over situation. My body was ejected from the Blazer and was found a hundred and fifty feet from the vehicle. (I do not know what happened to the seat belt but this is what happened.) The impact caused my back to be pushed from the middle of my body to one side and, as a result, the spinal cord was damaged, causing me to be paralyzed from the waist down. The ambulance took me to Pontiac Osteopathic Hospital first. It was there that they stabilized me and then sent me to Beaumont Hospital in Royal Oak. Because my wallet was thrown from my body the police did not know my identity and thus could not contact my family. When I did not come home or call, my wife became worried. She began to call various hospitals at random. The first one she called was Pontiac Osteopathic. They said that they had someone of my description there and it did not look good.

My wife called the church that we attend. My pastor, Dominic Russo, and Associate Pastor James Sutherland came, along with a friend, Willy Westly. They all prayed for me, and I believe that it was their prayers, and the prayers of many who had heard of the crash and were praying, that made a dramatic difference in me staying here on Earth or going to Heaven. I'm not sure how it all works, but I believe at that moment God heard the prayers of His people on my behalf. I have to say that Heaven would have been easier than what I have had to go through and some days I wish I would have gone. I'm seeing more and more that I'm here for a reason. We are all here for a purpose. The Apostle said, "For to me, to live is Christ and to die is gain" (Phil. 1:21). He goes on and says, "But if I live on in the flesh, this will mean fruit from my labor..." (Phil. 1:22). In other words, Paul understood that Heaven was real and better than Earth and to be there would be far greater, however being alive meant that he would be used by God and fruit would come from his labors. We are here by God's design and whether it's big or small in terms of fruit it all matters to God. You matter to God and even if your sphere of influence is big or small it does not matter; it is being faithful in your walk with God that is most important.

Leaving the store was the last thing I remembered until I woke up five days later on my way to get two twelve-inch titanium rods put in my back to support my back as a result of being severely broken. On my way to the operating room I woke up and heard my sister's voice: "Brad, you've been in a car accident and you broke your back." Immediately I thought, God is going deliver me and heal me like He has in the past. He will heal me.

Before I go into detail about my injuries and recovery process, I want to talk about the cause of my injuries, the woman who was driving drunk. She was, of course, prosecuted for this criminal offense. When the trial was going on (which was after I'd recovered sufficiently to participate), I was determined to go to all the proceedings. Mothers Against Drunk Driving (MADD) was also there with us to offer support and walk us through the process. Mark Barron was the prosecuting attorney; he also was a great support and was a key player in seeing that she got the maximum sentence. One of my physical therapy trainers at the time was telling me not to bother with being a part of the proceedings. He thought it was a waste of time and that time would be better spent in therapy than in the courthouse.

To this day I believe with all my heart that if I did not show up in my wheelchair and if MADD never showed up to support us, and my sisters, mom, wife and son did not write letters to the judge at the time of sentencing then the woman would not have even gone to jail. She would have been given a slap on the wrist. If we did not go up to Lansing for the parole proceedings she would have gotten out within a year. The justice system thrives on involvement. For sure there are laws and those laws are enforced to a certain extent. However, the courts and the jails are overloaded, so the rationale is to release some of the "minor" offenses to make room for the major ones. The problem is that what one considers minor the other considers major. Drunk driving is, for many, a "minor" offense. To those like me who have been deeply affected by it, it is major.

The woman drunk driver hired an attorney who told her to plead temporary insanity. She took some tests that were ordered by the state, which she failed. She was not insane; she was drunk. This one drunk driver cost the State of Michigan (the taxpayers) thousands of dollars in court fees. The insurance company paid out millions in medical costs, and I have been given a life sentence. This is only one drunk driver. There are an average of eighteen thousand people killed every year on the streets of this nation by drunk drivers.

I wondered about the woman that hit me. At one of the first court hearings we went to I saw her. I did not feel anger or rage toward her. I think because I was just trying to survive that I had little energy to be angry. My wife was upset, which was totally understandable. When I was leaving the courtroom, though, the woman let the door close on me when I was in my wheelchair. This was the kind of person she was. I look forward to one day speaking to her to see if she understands what she has done to me and the pain she has caused my family. Most of the people in the legal field who know her have told me that they are amazed by the lack of remorse that she demonstrates about the whole situation. People ask if I'm bitter. I say I don't have time, I'm just trying to get better. The woman has problems and I hope she gets the help that she needs. I hope one day to lead her to Jesus.

After being stabilized, I spent two weeks in the intensive care unit (ICU) and an additional five weeks in rehab in the hospital. Slowly, I started to come back. The crash left me with a closed-head injury, my spleen was removed, my ribs and vertebra were cracked and worst of all, and I had a spinal cord injury (SCI). The spinal cord carries the signal from the brain to the rest of the body. It branches off from all points down the back and sends the signal to the rest of the body to do what the brain says, including the involuntary things like breathing. My level of injury was not as high as Christopher Reeves. His was a high cervical injury, which means that it was close to the brain stem, which is why he needed a ventilator to help him breath. Mine was a "thoracic 8," or "T8," which is about the middle of the back. Cervical is from the brain stem down seven vertebrae, then thoracic in the middle and toward the rear end is the lumbar and the lowest part of the back is the sacral. Seven cervical vertebrae, twelve thoracic, five lumbar, and five sacral. Picture it like a river with many small streams that are coming off it. When there is an SCI, it is like a big slab of concrete falls right in the middle of the river and stops the flow of water. Scar tissue forms after the injury and creates the barrier in the spinal cord. This scar tissue must be removed and then some sort of bridge put in so the nerves can reconnect. Much work is being done in this area and many are hopeful for a cure soon.

I do not remember much from when I was in ICU, and the things I do remember were not even real, they were in my mind as a result of the medication I was on. I remember arguing with the Canadian government on a street in Canada and sleeping under a desk in a different room that they had moved me to. There was, of course, no Canadian government and I was in the same room the whole time. It is funny how your dreams or thoughts true or not, real or not, and can leave a stronger impression than what you go through physically. I remember very little of what was actually going on, but I do remember some things like the male nurses and the hockey playoffs. I don't remember what the nurses looked like, only their voices. Vivid in my mind, though, is the Canadian government and the episodes under the desks. When you're on medication your mind will play tricks on you.

The recovery process was, and is, long and hard. After the 9-11 attacks, the twin towers of the World Trade Center came down in less than an hour, but to rebuild them would take years. My body was broken, and yet I had the belief that God would come through and heal me. The night of the accident my friend Carl, who is a doctor, told me that on the way to the hospital that he works at he was "arrested" by the Lord to pray. He did not know for whom or why, but he obeyed and prayed. He told me that the burden lifted from him at the same time that I stabilized. My other friend James said he prayed against the "spirit of death" that was seeking to take me. I was between the two worlds; however I did not see any bright lights or great visions. I saw nothing and heard nothing. (If I did I could be on the circuit telling my story!) The way I see it is that this injury can't be like Paul's "thorn in the flesh" (2 Cor. 12:7), to keep me from exalting myself, because there were no tremendous revelations. Just darkness.

My sisters, mom, wife and kids along with many people from the church, including many preachers that my pastor knew, came and prayed for me and gave me great encouragement. People from work took up offerings and gave them to my wife for food or whatever else was needed. So much support came from my friends at Oakland Christian Church that I could write pages, thoughtful, practical things like bringing meals and sending money. My father in-law, whom I love, came and prayed and literally wept over me while I was in ICU. I know for a fact that I would not be here without the many prayers and support. At the time I could not really read the Bible much because of all the medication and weakness. God sent men and women to read for and pray with me. It was amazing.

After the two weeks in ICU, I was shifted to a waiting room to continue to recover and wait for a place in the rehab unit. That room was a real challenge. I could not sit up, and they kept trying to get me up and make me do things. I was coughing and throwing up and, at the time was mentally not really with it. I do not remember much, only that every one was nice and I felt that they were really trying to help. Finally, I was shifted to the rehab unit.

Bill and Essie Stamper, who were friends of mine, came to see me and they were really encouraging me to trust God. They were the first of a long line of people who came to see me over the next five weeks. My days were really busy, and I found myself ministering to many people as I was also receiving ministry. One of my best friends in Michigan at the time was going through a divorce. I felt really bad for him, his wife and kids. He came to see me and wept at my bedside about his situation. I was able to pray for him, but have only seen him a couple times since the crash.

Brandon was about sixteen when I met him at the hospital. He and his buddies were in one of his friend's cars and were hit by a car just outside the neighborhood. His was not a spinal cord injury but a brain injury. His mind only came back partially. I became close with his dad, Kevin, and still keep in touch with him. People have said to me, "at least you still have your mind," and the more I see people who have brain injuries, the more I agree. Outside of a miracle, Brandon is not likely to have a normal life. Every day, I was made more aware of the plight of so many. Husbands and wives were being discharged not because they were ready but because the insurance said so. It didn't matter if they were judges, principals, or laborers, or whether they were rich or poor. I was being educated, and it was not a course I had signed up for.

A few days before I was discharged they sent me down to a part of the hospital where they check your eyes. While I was in the office, I was moving from one room to the next and I must have pushed the wheelchair a little too hard; the chair fell over backwards and my head missed the door jam by an inch. I was so upset that I told my wife, "If the Devil is going to take me let him finish the job!" So much is going through your mind that you do not even understand at the time; all you know is that you want things to be normal again. But you fear they never will be.

I really felt like this was not going to be my life, that I would beat this and I would rise and walk again. One of my nurses, Ken, was a Christian, and we would get into talks about the Bible and church. I would challenge him about different issues, and he would tell me about his situation as a teacher in the church fighting against tradition versus what the Bible really says. "Go with the Word," I would tell him. He was a great blessing. Another nurse, Marie, introduced me to a guy she had met a few months before, named Adam. Adam and his mom and sister came to see me in the hospital. He had been in a crash with his best friend. He was driving drunk, his friend was killed in the wreck, and he was left with an SCI. He came with yellow roses, a sign of hope, and encouraged me to not give up or listen to the doctors if they were saying you would never walk. To this day, not one of the doctors I've had has ever told me I would never walk. The surgeon explained to me what happened. My spine was pushed to one side and then returned, like a spring, but it was damaged in the process and did not go back all the way. He told me if anyone would walk it would be me. At the time, you're just thinking that I *will* get up, and that focus occupies your mind. I can say that all my experiences in the hospital were positive and all the people I met were encouraging.

I'm a typical guy; in many ways my hormones are affected by the sight of my eyes. My wife is beautiful, and I'm attracted to her and committed to her.

Some of the nurses and aides were nice and helpful, and some were pretty. They were not only tending to my needs, but were lifting me up and putting me in bed and also helping me take a shower. Some of them were also assigned to help me go to the bathroom, which is humiliating and disruptive to the male ego. At the time you just keep telling yourself, this is temporary. I've heard guys joke about nurses and how they were attracted to them, but I had no desire whatsoever for them. I was thankful for their help, but my heart was still toward the Lord, and when my wife would come to see me she looked better than all of them anyway. Looking at her in the mornings when she came gave me a renewed sense of motivation to keep going. She, more than anyone was, and is, my biggest help and cheerleader. So much was happening during those days. A whole new world was opening to me and my family that was somewhat disturbing: the world of rehab and insurance.

You've heard the saying it is not what they tell you but what they don't tell you. It's never truer than in the case of catastrophic injury. When all the doctors would gather around for meetings to discuss my case, I commended them for their help and support. For the most part, I believe people in the healthcare system want to help.

When I was finally discharged I was given a "case manager." They are there to "manage the case," help you with your needs, and guide you through the maze of this new world. The insurance company issued us a case manager in the beginning. We did not know that we had a choice to pick our own case manager, so we went with the one they gave us. While I was in the hospital they "let us" have a car so I could get out into the community. The adjuster said that we had to return it each night to the rental place. We did, until we realized that it didn't matter, because the cost was the same if we would have kept it.

This was the beginning of a push to get us on their turf, to go by their rules, right from the get go. We called her the "Adjuster from Hell," and I truly believe she was led by the Devil. She really terrorized us, and tried to make us feel as if we had no rights and that we were subject to them and their rules. You buy insurance for this reason, to insure you in case you are hurt.

I finally left the hospital and began the real recovery process at home. In the state of Michigan, a spouse or caretaker are entitled to "attendant care benefits." Your spouse or caretaker would get paid so much per hour for every hour he or she took care of you. This, along with providing transportation and accessible housing is part of the state law. They do not tell you this and we had to find out for ourselves over time. At the hospital they did not "let us" have a car; they were obligated by law to do so. In fact if you are catastrophically injured you have a right to unlimited rehab for the rest of your life, as well as transportation and accessible housing. They don't tell you that, though. They would be totally happy if you would take your wheelchair and sit in a corner and die, and the sooner the better. This sounds harsh, I know, and not all insurance adjusters are like this, but the trend in the insurance world is moving in this direction. This is why good lawyers are necessary.

It always amazes me that the healthcare system would go to all the time and expense to help you get your life back when you're in the hospital, but when you get out, the rules change. In many ways, you feel deserted and you wonder about it all. Most people will never have to deal with this, thankfully, and most will only hear about the "system" in broader economic terms. I do believe there are solutions to every problem and there is for this one. As complex as it is, it can find order. I pray it changes, and I believe it will.

When I left the hospital they set me up at a rehab clinic that was connected to the hospital where I stayed. They told me I had a choice about where I could have rehab but didn't give me any choices other than the one connected to the hospital. While I was there, my wife and I both felt funny about the whole thing. They wanted to see if I could get up off the floor onto the wheelchair and, because of my broken shoulder they would "assist" me up off the floor and put me in the chair, and then tell me how well I did. I can't even lift myself up now after all these years and my scapula is healed–how could I have done it then? But this was a push to say I lifted myself up so they could sign me off and tell the insurance company that, if I did fall out of my chair, I could get up.

Later they wanted me to sign papers indicating that I no longer needed their service. They were having meetings without me, which was against the law (in Michigan you and your case manager are to go to these meetings in order to keep things honest). My case manager at the time went without me because she was a part of the system, and to us, the whole thing just didn't seem right. Again, at the time, I did not fully understand Michigan's no-fault insurance laws, but in the months to come, I would learn. After they tried to get me to sign the papers, I called my attorney and he supported me leaving as soon as possible, so I did.

After some searching, we ended up in Flint, Michigan at McClaren Spinal Cord Recovery and Rehabilitation. It was more than thirty miles from our house and a real pain to drive to three times a week, but we did. They were more sympathetic, but still in the pocket of the insurance company in many ways. They gave me ultrasound for my shoulder and put me in a tilt table. A tilt table is a padded table that you lie on horizontally; then, you're strapped down and it tilts so you are upright. The "ultrasound" is a machine that sends ultrasonic waves to the injury site that accelerates healing. Both were of great help.

Early on, I realized that in order to get up I was going to need braces. I was asking my doctor for leg braces, as I really felt that this was the next step. I urge every spinal cord patient to get braces and stand up as soon as possible. While I was at McClaren, George, the physical therapist (PT), helped me to stand up with braces in between parallel bars. I was actually able to use my legs standing and walking with these braces. The problem was that the braces that he used on me were about twenty-five years-old and cut the back of my leg. The leg braces that the doctor gave me a prescription for were not being approved by the Adjuster from Hell. I thought, who is running the show? How can an adjuster deny a basic need like this? No one seemed too outraged by this and the PT and doctor were hands-off about the situation. The leg braces cost over seven thousand dollars, which explained the delay. Finally, after more than a year of waiting we bought them ourselves and waited for reimbursement, which took months.

This is how they operate. Every time a hospital or doctor's office would call the Adjuster about something surrounding my case she would yell and scream. Everyone who was associated with my case who came in contact with her all said the same thing: "What's up with her?" My present doctor told me that he has seen a lot of nasty adjusters but she was the worst. Totally unreasonable. At a meeting in my house with my attorney, case manager, the Adjuster from Hell, and her boss, after I finished telling everyone why I needed the leg braces she asked, "Why do you need the braces?" My attorney responded, "Because he doesn't want to sit on his a–! He just told you!"

If you're in this kind of situation, or know someone who is struggling with these things at all, you must get an attorney and you must fight or you will be relegated to the "back of the bus," so to speak. Christopher Reeves talks about this in his book *Nothing is Impossible*: "During negotiations with our insurance carrier we discovered the main reason patients are routinely denied even the essentials, only thirty percent fight back. Since seventy percent of their policy holders are easily intimidated, there is no upside for compliance. Moral responsibility does not drive the insurance industry. Threatened lawsuits are often necessary to get results." Seventy percent of people give up fighting and therefore do not get what they are entitled to. I'm telling you the truth, these disability and injury lawyers on TV sound like shysters, but many are just trying to help. Find someone you can trust, and don't stop looking until you find the right one. Some are bad, but some are not.

When you have physical pain it affects every part of your being and though there are things you can take to help, in many instances there are nasty side effects from these medications. In my case, I would take something to help the pain, but when it wore off the pain would come back worse than if I had not taken anything. Early on they gave me a pain patch. These patches are a narcotic, which means they are powerful and addictive. They start with a high dose, and you're supposed to cut the amount as the pain goes away. The pain was massive. It was like someone putting a hundred pound pack on my back and standing on it. It is hard to describe the intensity of the pain, but these patches really did help. At first, I applied them every three days. They would last about a day and a half then the pain would come back strong. In my mind I knew I needed to get free from these drugs, so I tried to work through the pain and not increase the dose.

It occurred to me after a while that I had a choice: was I going to keep taking it and probably have to increase the dose, or quit it altogether? I chose to stop taking it, and I shook and sweat for three days withdrawing, but when it was over the pain was more manageable. When the pain would come back I would take something, but I would not make it a habit. I do not condemn anyone for taking pain pills, but I do encourage anyone to not make a habit of it and to try to get off of them as soon as possible. The body can and will heal itself, and there are mechanisms in us that fight pain, though it takes time. The time thing is the hardest to deal with.

Take medication for a season until you have developed enough strength to fight it on your own. Try different supplements and see if your body responds to any. I spent a lot of time researching various natural ways to fight pain, good foods, rest, and training in particular. It is vital to get the right kinds of food and enough activity and rest. I struggled with the whole rest thing, feeling guilty for sleeping, but I've come to realize that sleep is not the enemy. God made sleep for a reason, and it is a good thing, but like everything else, we have to balance it out with eating and activity and find just the right amount. Whenever you're going though any intense changes you will require more sleep. If you're seriously injured or just fighting certain pain, this is the only long term solution that I know of. I still fight pain every day since the crash. It has receded some, but still it is an everyday battle.

There are two kinds of pain, emotional and physical. The physical is just pain in the body from some outside source. Like a cut or some contact with a fist or a baseball bat. We all pretty much understand physical pain. Emotional or mental pain is a little more difficult to define. It is hurt of the heart or the emotions. It is inward agitation that may have valid reasons or may not. I think that emotional pain is easier to deal with than chronic physical pain. Chronic physical pain makes you focus on it alone; it's all you can think about. Like stubbing your toe. For those moments you forget about everything else. Emotional pain is harder to pinpoint. We all have emotional pains on some level, but not all have intense physical pain.

These two are different and yet pain is something that causes us to try various things that we would not normally try, for example, different medications or methods of healing. I have been on a crusade these past years to conquer my pain. My reasoning is, that if I'm in great pain, then I will not be any help to anyone. So rather than just sit in pain, I have done all that is in my power to defeat it without using prescription drugs. I still use some medications, but I feel that it is under control.

The pain was intense at every level and the Adjuster from Hell was adding to it on a daily basis. My wife was extremely distressed by her, but I had faith that God was going to do something. At one point I felt that the Lord was going to remove her. I told my wife and a couple of other people I felt she would be removed off the case. About five days later, for some reason, my wife picked up the phone to call the Adjuster from Hell. We never called down there, and really should not because we had an attorney, and he was supposed to deal with her. But for some reason, that day my wife called and got her voice mail: "This is _____; I am no longer with_____ __ Insurance..." There was a spirit of rejoicing in the house. My wife called others to tell the good news. "Ding dong the witch is dead," the pool therapist said. She caused us great harm, and God removed her. David talked about God dealing with his enemies in the book of Psalms, and I know we can trust God to deal with our enemies as long as we are on the side of truth. Sometimes we need to ask for the "Alexander the coppersmith blessing" (Paul said that Alexander did him much harm and that God would deal with him, 2 Timothy 4:14). I do not know what happened to the Adjuster from Hell, nor do I question. This was the breakthrough we needed.

The world of insurance and heath care is extremely complex, and as I've said, for the most part, there are many good people in the system who want to help. They are bright people who have applied themselves to education and the process of becoming useful in helping others. Doctors go to school for years and apply themselves for countless hours and pay out thousands of dollars in order to become effective in helping others. This is why it is absurd for an insurance adjuster to make decisions for a patient. And this happens a great deal.

The insurance companies have earned their reputation and this needs to be said. Many companies hire the coldest-hearted people in order to keep costs down. The greed and gouging take place on all levels and there needs to be a system of checks and balances, but people are people not just commodities. When a person buys a policy to insure himself, he expects that he will be taken care of. When doctors write out prescriptions in order to help one of these people, and the 'script is denied for no reason, this is an outrage. And when a pair of braces costs over seven thousand dollars, it seems way out of whack– and it is. This is the nature of the business, and if you or your loved one ever become subject to it, know your rights and be willing to fight for them. I used to try to think about keeping costs down for the insurance company, but now, if I know I need it and it is within my rights to receive it, I will fight for it, whatever it is. In other words, I can't worry about the cost of braces if I need them–that's not my job. If you're catastrophically injured, don't worry about the cost–get what you need. It's your right.

Chapter Ten

There Is A "God-Purpose"

I want to talk about pain again. Pain is a weird thing. I've experienced different kinds of pain since the crash. Nerve pain, for example, which is a burning, tingling pain, like pins and needles, times a hundred. My legs are still full of this kind of pain. Back pain, like someone pushing their fingernails into your back, from the inside, with a hundred-pound pack strapped tightly around your waist, from your belly button up to your chest. I also have had a stabbing pain in my ribs. They put shots of steroids in it, to no avail. It is a stabbing pain that is constant and is only stopped when I lay down and sometimes not then. My scapula was broken so my shoulder rubs against itself, and this causes much pain when I move my arm. Everyday I fight pain, which is the way it goes with many SCI people. Some have no pain, but most have a lot.

People, in general, live with many pains. Depression and despair are hard emotions to deal with when things are not going well. There is a grieving process to all losses that needs to happen. For some it's longer than others, depending on what the loss is. Every day, I had to pray for two hours just to get myself adjusted to what happened. I had entered the school of suffering, and in each class there was a hard professor. I did not know what to expect each day, but I committed each day to God. I read and prayed most days. People were a blessing, but as time goes on and you're out of the hospital, they figure everything is okay now and life goes on. And it does. But for me, the struggle was just beginning in many ways.

It seems in some ways life is a continuous series of losses. We lose many things as we grow, and it's difficult to deal with loss. No one wants to lose, but it's inevitable we will eventfully lose loved ones and friends to disease and death. Big corporations will lose profits. We lose in many ways at various times. Some lose limbs or eyesight or hearing. Life has phases, and with losses, there are some gains. We may lose our youth but gain maturity. We may not be able to compete at a certain sport at the same level when we get older, but maybe we may enjoy it more. Paul said, "I have suffered the loss of all things and count them as rubbish that I may gain Christ" (Phil. 3:8). He's talking about losing something but gaining something greater in return.

Losing my ability to walk is harder than any other emotional pain I have ever felt. When we lose, it affects our emotions; our emotions are a part of us, and in many ways, they control us. Job lost his family first, then his health. This was two-fold pain. His response was, "Though you slay me, yet will I trust You," and "Naked I came from the womb and naked I shall return. The Lord gives and the Lord takes away, blessed be the name of the Lord" (Job 2:21,13:15). The loss of family (emotional/mental pain) was followed by the loss of his health (physical pain).

I have not lost my family, so I don't know what that is like. I have lost many that were close to me, but these were older and those who would naturally leave this world. I really can't say how losing my kids would affect me because it has not happened. My son Paul was almost killed in a car accident but thankfully was spared. He had a closed-head injury and the whole side of his head was cut open and repaired by the surgeon. But with death of a loved one, time has to pass and healing must work its work. There is a grieving process to all these types of losses, and it is the natural mechanism that is in us to grieve through losses. The fact that I could not walk was one thing, but the everyday pain was another.

The physical pain was like adding insult to injury. Dealing with it day after day was almost all-consuming, then I also was forced to deal with the emotional side of it. Going out in public for the first time was so difficult. Having to experience people seeing me in a wheelchair got to me in a big way. I know a young guy, injured in a car wreck, who has a SCI, would not go out in public for almost three years. It's nothing to be ashamed of, but it just feels wrong. Having to constantly look up at people when you're in a conversation and not being able to sit in regular seats at games or school events takes a while to get used to.

For a young man who is not married this can be devastating in terms relating to the opposite sex. I encourage young guys in this situation to do everything in their power to get up with braces, eat right, take vitamins, take only medications that are totally necessary, and–most of all–don't lose hope. You are more than a body; you are a soul, and your life has as much value as it always has. I have seen life beat good people down.

Life is hard. If you're going through something, whether it is a physical or emotional pain, recognize that you can't make it on your own. Cry out to the God that is near and then do everything in your power to help yourself. I used to think I didn't want to live that bad, and that my life didn't have any real meaning. But, as a result of this injury, I see that I really *do* want to live, and life *is* worth it. It doesn't feel like that every day, but more and more it is getting better. Let time and the power of God help you make it to the next place in your heart. Don't give in to the pressure to find other ways out of your pain. God loves you and has a purpose for your life. Really.

We have to believe there is a purpose for everything under heaven. Nothing happens to us that does not first come through the hand of God. It has to "pass his desk," so to speak. If it comes through His hand, then it has a purpose. Paul says that "all things work together for the good of those who love God" (Rom.

8:28). He did not say *some* things, but *all*. What does "all" mean? It means "all!" When people ask why God allows suffering, in many ways it is the wrong question. The primary question should be "what is the purpose of life?" Then the other questions come into a better focus. So, if I believe that God is in total control of all things and bad things happen, then they must have a design, a reason.

I have heard people rage against simple common sense and then blame God for all the problems in the world. Why the AIDS epidemic? Simple: promiscuity. If men and women were committed sexually to each other for a lifetime, AIDS would slowly pass away. Who could not argue that if man were to run his life by the Ten Commandments that the world would be a different place? Jesus said that "to love the Lord with all your heart, mind, body and strength and to love your neighbor as yourself are the embodiment of the commandments. Upon these rest all the Law and the prophets" (Matt. 22:37-40). Modern technology is helping us live longer and better lives and yet suffering is a universal issue that will not go away. One hundred years from now there will still be suffering, and the question will go on being asked. The answer will still be the same: it is the wrong question. Right question: what is the purpose of life? Answer that, and suffering looks totally different.

One of the main things I have noticed about Satan and his ways is that he always wants to move us away from the central truth that God loves us and is *for* us, not against us (Rom. 8:31). That may sound elementary and cliché, but it is sometimes the things we take for granted that trip us up. Back to the basics. As I have been doing my best to recover from this injury with faith and work, I have had to fight the feeling deep inside, "why are you not totally healed? God really doesn't like you all that much, or God is punishing you for your hidden sins." Guilt sneaks up on you and brings you quickly into depression and despair. For many this is just as difficult as the actual emotional and physical pain that is a result of the tragedy. My mother-in-law died of a brain tumor, and right before she lost the ability to really think and reason with her mind, her one question was, "Why?" The main theme of the book of Job is about his agony of the "why" of it all. God comes through in the end, but some scholars say it was five to ten years before things changed for Job.

Pain makes you do things you would not normally do. It moves you in a direction that you would not normally move in. Job went from being a pillar in the community and a prime example of a godly man to a man whose breath was repulsive to his wife. But God is always looking at the heart. Pain moved Job from being a man who was rich and strong to a man who was secluded and weak. Man looks on the outward appearance but the Lord looks on the heart (1 Sam. 16:7). God is always looking at what is going on inside when things are falling apart on the outside. The eyes of the Lord range though out the whole world looking to support a man who is totally committed to Him (2 Chron. 16:9). To support his heart, the inner man. The seat of the mind, will and emotions. It is, in essence, who we are. We are complex beings with many different aspects to ourselves including our body, mind, heart, will and emotions. We have appetites for food, for relationships, for marriage, family and recreation. We have needs to be productive, and we want to do well and yes, prosper. Pain becomes an interference to these desires. It says to us "I want your attention, I want to change you." It is our response that is crucial.

God allowed Job to be attacked outwardly, but God was looking inwardly at his *heart*. Job's words and actions followed his heart. Again, the Lord rebuked him for his lack of understanding, but He saw his heart from the beginning. Job's response reflected who he was inside. You can fool others with words and works and even try to fool yourself, but God is looking to the core of who you are and it is in that place that He seeks purity and communion (Heb.12:14). "Blessed are the pure in heart, for they shall see God (Matt. 5:8). Your heart is who you are really. It is the place the Lord resides if you're a believer (Eph. 3:17). The Devil has been allowed to attack, God's people but only for God's purposes. God is sovereign, and He has a timing in which to deliver His own when He chooses. You can do good things with a wrong heart, but with a pure heart you will be supported by the Lord and approved by Him. In fact, *only* He is able to make our hearts pure. Job was delivered in the end and was approved by God.

Martin Luther said the Devil is the "ape of God." He is only allowed to go so far. Before my accident, we had two Border Collies, Jake and Frankie. We had Jake first, and then a couple years later (against my will), my wife bought Frankie. I used to run with Jake and he would pull me and even though I jerked the leash it didn't matter, he would still pull and try to run ahead of me. I used to think Jake and I were a lot alike; I always felt like I was running ahead of God, like dragging God into my thing. The more a dog wants to run the more you have to cage him in.

In our old neighborhood, Jake would run away and, though it was heavily populated and cars were everywhere, he never got hit or was injured. When we moved out to the country we thought, now Jake can run a little more without as much fear of being hit. One day in February, I was home from work due to the weather. I worked construction outside and that particular day we couldn't work, so I decided to paint the trim in the basement we had finished. While I was doing that, my wife and kids were out side with the dogs and I heard Suzanne screaming. She came and told me that Jake was hit by a truck. I ran out and saw him lying on the street with his guts hanging out, lifeless. I ran up to the two ladies in the gas truck that had hit Jake and they seemed unconcerned. I called the company and asked if they would pay to have him removed or if the city would come out, and they said no to both questions.

I learned something about being in the country. You can't run away from problems, and if you're thinking all the people are really nice out in the country, you're wrong. Many of them are out in the country because they do not want to be bothered. How can you love your neighbor if you don't have one? The whole mentality of isolation is un-Biblical.

Anyway, for some reason, God preserved Jake while he ran in a busy suburb, but allowed him to be killed out in the country.

After Jake died we got a new dog, Alice, a Fox Terrier. It was a small dog but it had a lot of spunk. Frankie would love to chase the tennis ball so I would take the lacrosse stick and throw the ball way out in the yard and she would chase it down, pick it up with her mouth and bring it back. We would do this for a long time until she wore out. Alice was a lot like Jake, she wanted to run away, so we would have to chain her up in the front yard on a leash about twenty feet long. So when I would throw the ball to Frankie, Alice would run after the ball also, only she was chained up. When she reached the end of the chain her rear end would fly up in the air in the direction she was going and she would hit the grass and then pop up ready for more. I used to laugh at her, it was quite comical. She wasn't too bright, so she would do it over and over.

I believe the Devil is like this; he is on a chain and can only go so far. How far he is allowed to go is in God's hands. At times we must resist him and, at other times, we must concede that God has allowed this thing in our lives for a purpose and trust God for the lessons He wants us to learn and realize that it is all designed to make us more like Him. The Devil can only go so far and no further. And everything that God allows is for the express purpose of making us like Jesus. This is not a natural way to look at things, and part of us screams against it. That's why the Scriptures say we must be "transformed by the renewing of our minds (Rom. 12:2). We need a spiritual mind to see things the way they really are. In many ways, my eyes were being opened.

This story in the Bible illustrates another dimension of the spiritual world around us. One day, Elisha and his servant were surrounded by enemy forces (2 Kings 6:13-18). His servant was afraid and told Elisha that they were about to be destroyed, so Elisha asked God to "open his eyes." He saw that they were surrounded by chariots of fire. Greater were the forces with them than the enemy around them. But it takes God to help us to see this on a constant basis. In our human state, we are not able to access or see this dimension most of the time. The Devil and his imps are every where in the spirit world but we don't see them all the time (or at least I have never met anyone who consistently sees demonic forces, though I have met men whom I respect who deal with demonic forces). However, we see the effects of the Powers of Darkness everyday, just watch the news.

We do have a place in fighting evil in all its forms, and the armor is provided (Eph. 6:10-20). We are told to be strong in the Lord and in His mighty power, to "take up the shield of faith that is able to extinguish all the flaming missiles of the evil one." Faith is a good thing, not a club to hammer us (as in, "you don't have enough faith" or "you're suffering because of your lack of faith"), but a catalyst to bring us to God. Faith doesn't really do anything but tap into what is already there. Faith didn't die on the cross for you or create spiritual things. Jesus already died on the cross and the Spirit is already poured out on all flesh, so our faith embraces these truths and in turn they become a reality in our lives.

People in every religion pray and have faith. The World Trade Center bombings are rooted in the faith of young men who believe that Allah is God and Muhammad is his prophet. They say "go and slay the infidel; much reward awaits you if you die for Allah." This faith is not the kind of faith that will save your soul, and yet it is real faith; the object, though, is wrong. Job had faith to believe that God was God no matter what. He did not waver, but like Abraham, he grew strong in faith and, in the end, God restored and blessed him (James 5:11). There is a general warfare that is ongoing, and there are times when, at God's discretion, the Devil is used to carry out God's purpose.

Peace, love, and joy flow from God to the heart of the believer. The main theme of Ecclesiastes is that you cannot be happy without God. You can work, give your life to pleasure, commit adultery, and have unlimited sexual pleasures, and in all these you will not attain real joy, because true joy is from God. "The joy of the Lord is my strength" (Neh. 8:10). "Fear God and keep His commandments, this is the chief purpose of man (Eccl. 12:13). For by entering into that, a person will love God and enjoy Him forever. Stimulation and gratification of the five senses will only bring a temporary relief from your vain life, Solomon says.

Grace is all about God's favor, unmerited and undeserved. The little baby that has done nothing is the object of God's favor. The man who is old and falling apart is the object of God's love. Not because of anything they have done, but simply because God cannot help Himself to love, because He *is* love (1 John 4:7). This may seem elementary, but many Christians who have been saved many years still struggle with this very concept: Does God really love me?

I recommend John Piper's books, *Desiring God* and *The Pleasures of God*. In these works, Piper talks about the fact of God's perfect happiness at being God. In *Desiring God*, he writes, "The chief end of God is to glorify God and enjoy Himself forever." He needs no outside stimulation to be happy. He is happy in Himself. A true seeker of God is really a "Christian hedonist," in that he realizes that God, being totally happy in Himself, does not need me, but I need Him, and He is able to make and keep me happy. I seek Him as the ultimate source of pleasure (Ps. 16:11).

I find it difficult to believe that, after my dramatic salvation experience, I would ever doubt the love of God or think that I can gain His favor by works, but I have struggled with these thoughts all my life. Works are good, but you can't gain God's favor by them. Your life is hid with Christ in God (Col. 3:3). All spiritual blessings are yours, regardless of your level of faith (Eph. 3:3). If you had faith to believe for salvation and received a divine assurance that your sins are forgiven then you have faith. Your faith came by hearing the truth of the gospel (Rom. 10:17).

At a point in time your fallen will was awakened to see the truth, and at that point, you had the ability to believe. All able people (those who are not retarded mentally) have "response-ablity," that is, ability to respond to the truth. God could not justly damn a person who he deemed incapable of believing. Some (Calvinists) say that you are given faith to believe due to election (God electing you to salvation). However, though I can see many reasons for this belief, it seems to take away man's part, and therefore puts God in the seeming position of being unfair. God is not unjust, and yes, He does choose ("Jacob I loved and Esau I hated") but that is according to His eternal perspective. In other words, God knows what everyone will do because in His economy, everything has happened. He doesn't make the person believe or keep believing, but He knows who will. The issue is we don't know, so we must keep believing in all circumstances.

God sees the end from the beginning. He knows everything about everything all the time. With Him there is no time. He knows who will be saved, but still allows the person to choose and once he chooses (which is an act of his will) the individual is given the Spirit of God as divine assurance of his faith. It takes God to know God or love God. In our depraved state, we need something to enable us to believe without forcing us. That's why the Apostle said, "Knowing the terror of the Lord, we persuade men" (2 Cor. 5:11). Men can be persuaded, by word and deed, and that is our job here. Our faith is a means to an end, and the end is God. True faith is based on God and not on itself. Faith in faith will not suffice. Faith is not an emotion or even a mental decision. Faith comes to us by hearing, and it affects our mind, will and emotions. It comes by hearing, and hearing by the Word of God.

So then, the more you truly know of God and His character through His Word, the stronger your faith becomes. We are so prone to do and not believe, that is why how-to books sell. Just tell me what to do. And God answers, "nothing." That is, nothing in your own strength (Luke 10:38-42). Mary and Martha, who are sisters, are at their home with Jesus. Martha is all about serving (which is good) and Mary is all about Jesus and His words (which is better). He said, "Mary had chosen that good part, which will not be taken from her." I want to encourage you if you feel out of it and that you are not being used or fulfilling your purpose, keep waiting on Him.

He will be faithful to His Word. He will give you the desire of your heart. Rest in Him even when you don't want to rest, force yourself there. Find intimacy with God.

Chapter Eleven

God's Sovereignty and the Faith Struggle

Since the "Adjuster from Hell" left us, things have been better, for sure. But not perfect. We still have had various little battles to fight and, in my personal life, it seems like I'm still not truly settled. As I've already said, I've gone from a working-hard-playing-hard husband and father to someone who is struggling to just survive. I have had to discipline every area of my life. I have had to eat right (not that I was eating wrong before), train consistently, and rest more. I am still fighting pain, which has been a major issue. I have had to take certain medication and, hardest of all, I had to fight the feeling that if I just had the faith I would be healed.

Reading, praying and talking to friends have helped greatly. Since the crash, I have been in physical therapy five days a week. Prior to coming to the

Detroit Medical Center (DMC), I was a part of the "Recovery Project," started by Charlie Parkhill, who was injured in the ocean. He is a quad, who has been fighting for years to get back up on his feet. He and Polly Swingle, a physical therapist (PT) that I met at a rehab center in Novi, Michigan, began this company when they realized that the whole PT world was only designed to make someone "functional" in the wheelchair. They wanted to give people the opportunity for more aggressive therapy that was designed to help activate and stimulate what someone has in terms of muscles and nerves, rather than isolate people and tell them that they could only go so far.

This company along, with the DMC, are the only places in Michigan with an aggressive program like this. They have a "stim-bike," a cable harness and treadmill, along with other equipment. The stim-bike stimulates the muscles with electricity. As you are sitting with your feet strapped in the peddles your legs are activated with electricity to peddle. I've been doing this for over a year three times a week and just recently started walking on the treadmill being supported by a harness and cable. As you are supported, there are two people helping move your legs in a walking motion. These things, as well as being in the pool for swimming and massage, have, I believe, kept me on the cutting edge of the recovery process.

When I was first injured, I met a doctor from Ecuador who did surgery on the damaged part of the spinal cord by taking nerves from the legs and grafting them into the spine, hoping that the nerves would reconnect. At first I was going to have the operation, but a number of things discouraged me from it, and now I'm glad I did not. Lately I have been pursuing a surgical operation in Portugal similar to the one in Ecuador, but instead taking nerves from the leg the doctor takes olfactory cells (out of the nose) and implants them into the spine. The olfactory cells never stop reproducing and will adapt to where you put them. Alternative or experimental surgeries are out there, and I have explored many of them, and continue to do so.

The Miami Project is the most aggressive spinal cord research hospital in the country and is spearheaded by Nick Bonicontii who used to play for the Miami Dolphins. His son was injured and became a quadriplegic while playing football. Christopher Reeves has funneled millions into the program, and recently the Miami project has put together a "combination therapy" that has helped rats regain movement after being paralyzed. By injecting a recipe of cells into the spine these paralyzed rats regained movement in their legs.

The word to all who are paralyzed is to keep yourself in shape until there is a cure. There are many other groups doing various things, and just recently, right here in Detroit at the Detroit Medical Center, they are taking a more aggressive role in helping people with spinal cord injuries (SCIs). There are many doctors and supporters who are helping make the DMC one of the most aggressive SCI rehab programs in the nation. Many who have had no operations are coming for the physical rehab and are getting better. I have met people personally who have had both surgeries, those in Ecuador with the leg nerves and the olfactory cells from the nose in Portugal. None of the people that I have met who have had these procedures have any significant return in that they are not walking on their own. Again, so much is being done that gives us tremendous hope. These efforts are leading researchers in the right direction and many believe soon there will be a long term solution to paralysis.

Since the crash, many prayers have gone up for my healing. Even before I was injured, I used to think about the whole divine healing debate. I thought if I were ever sick or in a bad way, where would I rather be, in a place where they believed in healing or a place where they did not? I chose the former then and now. I went to an evening service at a faith church one of my friends invited me to. At the end of the service I went up for prayer. The elders laid hands on me and nothing happened. Later, while I was still there at the altar a young girl, about thirteen years-old came up to me and said that if I "would just get up out of the chair God would heal you." So I thought, God can use a young girl, He can use anything, so I put each arm around each of my two friends who were standing there and got up. As I stood for a few minutes my arms were getting tired, and I figured my friends were getting tired also, so I sat back down. I did feel that God did something but as far as a total healing, it did not come.

I'm more hesitant to go up to healing lines now, because I don't want to discourage others or myself.

I do think rolling up and then rolling back is disheartening for people. "What's wrong with that person or the ministry or God," they may think. When Jesus was walking on the water Peter said, "Master bid me come to You." Notice "to You." Peter didn't want theatrics, he wanted God (Matt. 14:27-33). When he heard the Master's voice, then he came. Not someone hoping to hear something; he heard God's direct voice. I feel worn out sometimes, trying to hear that Voice. Sometimes we want to hear it so bad we manufacture it in our own minds. Our mind plays tricks on us a lot.

Another time, a zealous sister in Christ told me at the end of a service the same thing. "If you would just stand up God would heal you." So I grabbed the pew and stood up, but really felt no strength in my legs. I have not given up believing, however these events have made me wonder. I believe God is in control, and faith can be tested (James 1:1-2). My faith would continue to be tested.

Why God waits to give certain things I don't know, He is the Boss. The Devil says "give up," but not God. I just heard about this man who had been incapacitated by a brain injury for ten years. He was not responding well at all, and then all of a sudden, he snapped out of it. He asked how long he had been out. When they told him it was ten years he was shocked; he thought it was only three months. Breakthrough and miracles can happen anytime or anywhere. God will not be confined to a box nor will He be forced by anyone to do anything against His will. He responds to earnest prayer, no doubt, and yet He will not be coerced. He is not surprised by the things that are happening in your life or the world as a whole. He is not playing "catch-up" with the Devil, He controls the Devil. The Lord is in heaven, and He does what He pleases (Ps. 115:3). Real faith will hold on, like Jacob, who said, "Lord, I will not let go until you bless me" (Gen. 32:26).

The widow wore out the unjust judge (Luke 18:1-2). Perseverance is imperative, but wisdom must be operative. We must first be convinced that the thing we are asking for is scriptural; is it in the Bible? Next, are we sure it is the will of God? If we ask anything according to His will, He hears us, and if we know that He hears us, "whatever we ask we know that we have the petitions that we have asked of him" (1 John 5:14-15). It says that Jesus saw what the Father was doing and did that. He saw the Father moving and went in that direction; He wants us to do the same (John 5:19).

Every prayer Jesus prayed was answered because He asked according to the Father's will. Sometimes, we ask things that are Biblically appropriate but are not God's will for that moment. This is where the rub is. Healing is in the Bible. Jesus healed the sick and told us to do the same, however many people are not healed that we pray for. Sometimes it is the timing. The beggar at the gate Beautiful was passed by the Lord, many scholars say, and yet the Apostles healed him (Acts 3:6-8). We can be sensitive to the Spirit of the Lord, but sometimes we have to admit we don't know. The best we can say is pray and believe, and, after that, trust that God's will will be done. I have struggled greatly by the lack of answers. Job waited for a long time. Can you imagine someone coming up to Job to pray the "prayer of faith" and when Job wasn't healed, telling Job, "see you don't believe enough?" In essence, this is what his friends said. Some argue that this was the Old Testament and now because we are living in the New Testament these types of lessons are not necessary; all should be healed by the prayer of faith. That is the reason we must rightly divide the Word of Truth. What does it say, what does it mean and how does it apply? As I said before, Satan is on a leash, and God has a hold of the leash. The question is how does the sovereignty of God fit in.

Gods's sovereignty is a subject that is taken out of context by many, it seems. On one hand there are those in certain camps that attribute everything to the sovereignty of God. "Well, it's just God's will that this has happened," the thinking goes. It happened, therefore, it must be God's will. I spoke at a victim's impact panel meeting for Mothers Against Drunk Driving, and it came to me that it is not God's will that a man lose his wife and two children to an out-of-control drunk driver who had four times the legal limit of alcohol in his blood and was speeding (which happened not too long ago, right by where I live). "Thou shalt not kill" is God's will, not "thou shalt kill." If an intruder comes to your house and wants to break in you must resist him and not allow him to come in. You don't just say, "come on in since you have come to steal, kill and destroy." You resist him and call 911. You may use your power and personal strength to resist him, say you have a gun or a bat or some other weapon. Or you may call a higher authority by summoning the police. This view states that whatever happens is God's will and we should not resist it, just accept it no matter what it is. Or if we do resist it for a season and bad still comes, then it is God's will.

The other view is the idea that we have the power over all things through prayer and the power of our words. God's sovereignty is subject to our words or confession. This too is a dangerous extreme. Back in the 1980s, this approach seemed to be widespread among the Pentecostal and Charismatic streams of Christianity. Things seem to have leveled out more, but there is still this thinking in many who remain in these streams. I have already alluded to this, but want to reinforce the truth of balance, because the truth is not in the extremes but is many-sided and in between the extremes.

The enemy of our soul is out to destroy our affections toward God. By one stream of thought, he tells a person God is distant and intimacy with Him is an absurd impossibility. You cannot really be intimate with a God that is light years away and has left us to ourselves down here on planet earth. So with the first idea that God has left us here, you may not be tempted to be bitter, but you will never achieve a close walk with Him (like Abraham who was a "friend of God") because it is impossible to be close with someone who is far away. On the other hand, the other concept of man's control through his words leaves a person bitter and angry or disillusioned when what he "commands" does not happen.

I have found it almost amusing how preachers will pray for a person or situation and if it doesn't go according to his word, you never hear them take any responsibility for it. But when you hear them from the pulpit, they insinuate that the blame must be placed on the individual. James says to call the elders of the church and the prayer of faith will save the sick (James 5:14-15). The idea stresses the prayer and faith of the elders to heal the sick. The person calls the elders, and it is the elders' faith that brings about the change. Jesus did tell his disciples to say to this mountain be removed and cast into the sea (Mark 11:22-24). This statement, though, is not a blanket statement to speak to any situation we don't like or any problem we have and instantly it will go away. I don't know about you, but I haven't seen many mountains moving around lately. You would think that someone would at least have seen one moving around.

This is not to disparage the idea of resisting the negative and embracing a positive faith-filled mental outlook. Paul said, "Whatever things are true, whatever things are noble, whatever things are just, whatever things are pure, and whatever things are lovely, whatever things are of a good report, if there is any virtue and if anything is praiseworthy-meditate on these things" (Phil. 4:8). He goes on to tell the Philippians to "Be anxious for nothing but in all things by prayer and petition make your requests known to God and the peace of God will guard your heart and mind in Christ Jesus (Phil. 4:6-7). Pray and believe, wait and trust. The famous "Serenity Prayer" by Reinhold Niebuhr states: "Lord help me to accept the things I cannot change, the courage to change the things I can, and the wisdom to know the difference." When bad things happen in our lives the first and natural thing is to try to fix it. The unnatural thing is to learn from God the real lesson and to make it a part of our lives.

"Work out your own salvation with fear and trembling for it is God who is at work both to will and to do for His good pleasure" (Phil. 2:12-13). Amazing. God says work it out, push through, don't despair when things don't go your way, have faith, and lean hard on Him. When David was in the caves hiding from Saul he found his joy in God (1 Sam. 24:1-23). There is no record of him saying, "Hey God, you said I would be king, and now I'm being hunted down by this demonized king." David had his moments of desperation and despair that he told God about (read the Psalms), but the thing he never forgot was his relationship with God when he was young, when he used to watch the sheep for his dad. That's where He found God, under the stars, alone. When he came against Goliath he said, I beat the lion and the bear this Philistine will be like them (1 Sam. 17:36). He fought his battles out in the wilderness with the sheep, but for him it wasn't about the battles won, but about God's presence. He said, "I want to behold Your beauty" (Ps. 27:4). Wow.

David saw something, and it started when he was young and it continued and matured when he was being run down by King Saul. "Thou I walk through the valley..." (Ps. 23:4). It's in the valley that true faith is expressed. Faith that is seen is not faith. If you have the thing that you are asking for you no longer need to seek or ask for it. Faith believes God in the valley without an answer to a specific prayer request. Since the crash, I have been asking in faith for healing, and I have seen certain things happen and feel that I am on my way to walk again, whether God heals me instantly or over time (or in heaven). But as I have already expressed, it has been a real struggle. If you're going through a hard time, I encourage you to seek and find God's presence.

I have been a Christian since August 20, 1977, and I can say that I would have never thought in a million years that I would be in this place mentally, physically and spiritually. I envisioned myself the next Billy Graham. I was going to change the world, and God was going to take care of me. I thought that when I graduated from college and got my master's degree, that doors would fly open, and I would be on my way. I thought that my preaching in the open air on college campuses would give me more not less opportunity, that it would be looked on favorably by the pastoral leaders, not negatively. All this was very difficult to take when things began to not work the way I thought they would. I could use this opportunity to blast the ministers who did not help a young preacher, or I could actually blame God for not coming through and letting all these bad things happen to me. I could curse the drunk driver for hitting me head on, on my way home from work.

I could blame myself (and, in fact, have done so at times) for my lack of maturity and inability to find God's leading.

Though I have said many things, the one thing I want you to take from all this is that faith in God is not about things going right in every way all the time. You have suffered, maybe more than I have, and are about to trash the whole God/faith thing, but don't. I urge you to wait on God and be of good courage (Ps. 27:14). To be still and know that He is God (Ps. 46:10). And to "fret not, it leads to evil doing" (Ps. 37:7-8). "Be anxious for nothing but in everything by prayer and supplication make your requests known to God" (Phil. 4:6-7). Know that it is about the heart and about your reaction to the whole storm that has come upon you. If you caused the storm, all the more, you must hold on and believe that God is with you and for you, and in time will turn things around (Rom. 8:28,31).

As a result of my years walking this walk, earnestly trying to seek God and do the right thing, I have concluded certain things, and some things remain to be answered. I have learned it's not about comparing and contrasting Dave Hunt with Kenneth Hagin, or John Wesley with Charles Finney, or standing with Hank Hanegraaff against many of them. It's about asking what does the Scripture say, what does it mean and what am I going to do about it? I have gained much learning from all these men, but the bottom line is what does the Scripture really say and mean and how does it apply. It's about doing justly, loving mercy and walking humbly with God (Micah 6:8), not just becoming a Bible scholar. Knowing that the purpose of the Scripture is to enable us to truly know God; it's not just about God. Some things are plain, like love your neighbor as yourself (Matt. 22:39). If we just do that, God would be pleased and many things would change. Other things are more difficult, as Peter explained, that some things that our beloved brother Paul wrote were difficult to understand that some distort to their own destruction (2 Peter 3:14-16). Truth must be grappled with and then concluded, even if that conclusion is that there is no conclusion.

In my physical and theological struggles, I have concluded some things can be answered and other things are left open to conclude. I have concluded that some things have no conclusion in this life. There is a mental world, a physical world and a spiritual world. They are all real and all are a part of the whole rhythm of life. Each one affects the other. You can't escape it. A man may deny that there is a God but sooner or later (hopefully sooner), he will see the Truth. Literally. You may deny the symptoms of your sickness and die an early death because you had "faith" to not call the doctor. The imbalance of your viewpoint has hurt you. You can be positive to the point where you deny reality.

I remember a man saying once, "You will always go in the direction of the most dominant thoughts that you allow in your mind." This is a true statement. However, if the dominant thoughts are based on a wrong premise, then you will go in a wrong direction. If you really believe that your words will control reality then you will go in that direction, but you will have to deny some reality along the way or just keep telling yourself that it is "in motion." If your house is on fire no amount of positive thinking will change it. Reality is hard for all of us to deal with. In my early years, I thought reality was about finding a utopian society through drug use and the hippie lifestyle, and that's the direction I went. Those were my dominant thoughts. Now though I try to keep my dominant thoughts on what I believe God said and is saying. Paul said to "test all things and hold fast to that which is good" (1 Thess. 5:21).

People are hurting and suffering on many different levels, and the church has not dealt too well on this issue, going from one extreme to the other. A.B. Simpson, a great man of faith that God used in healing, once said that if people are not healed instantly, "give them a blanket." It is important to work through these issues and make the necessary conclusions. God is good and He does have a plan for your life. It may not be the one you have planned, but nevertheless, it is His plan. The challenge is to commit each day to Him by faith, tomorrow is not and yesterday is gone. The only place that time touches eternity is in the present.

Truly, consider the birds, they do not struggle, nor the lilies of the field, they do not toil nor spin (Matt. 6:25-30). They just exist by the decree of the Lord. Being and doing are two different things. It is true that true doing comes out of true being, but doing can occur when the being is substandard. Most people are going through life not really living life; instead, they're always looking for the next event, the main focus being on tomorrow, or a year or ten years ahead, but failing to live in the moment. True being is the life of God in the soul of man, realized and experienced. To be fully alive is what is most important. "The glory of God is a person fully alive," said John Piper. "And God is most glorified, when we are most satisfied in Him." And to be truly satisfied inwardly by God and by knowing Him in reality is a wonderful pursuit.

C.S. Lewis said, "God screams to us in our suffering." I'm not sure if that's true all the time, because in my suffering I have felt totally abandoned. I have not felt the love of God, but I felt deserted and worse, I felt judged and condemned by men and God. I felt so much guilt and condemnation that when I would write in my journal all that came out was distress, not about my paralysis but about being rejected by God. Jesus, when on the cross said to the Father, "My God why have you forsaken me?"(Matt. 27:46). At His lowest point He felt that God had left Him. To get through this I would, each morning, pour out my broken heart to God. Sometimes it would take longer than other times, but my goal was to get through to the point where I could truly praise Him and sense His presence. Most of the time I did.

The Bible says that God is near to the broken-hearted and saves those who are crushed in spirit (Ps. 34:18,51:17). I have found Him in those times, though I have not always felt Him close, by faith I just accepted that He would never leave me (Heb.13:5). In my zeal to know Him and serve Him in many ways I have bypassed Him, thinking He was "out there" and not near. Always in the future but not in the present. Always reaching out for the remarkable and not just doing the thing at hand, believing that God is in the simple and the remarkable. If we only think that He is in the remarkable we will become depressed when we do not see the amazing. Oswald Chambers says in his devotional *My Utmost for His Highest*:

> "Arise and eat" (1 Kings 19:5). The angel did not give Elijah a vision, or explain the Scriptures to him, or do anything remarkable; he told Elijah to do the most ordinary thing, vis., to get up and eat. If we were never depressed we should not be alive; it is the nature of a crystal never to be depressed. A human being is capable of depression; otherwise there would be no capacity for exaltation. There are things calculated to depress, things that are the nature of death; and in taking an estimation of yourself, always take into account the capacity for depression. When the Spirit of God comes he does not give us visions, He tells us to do the most ordinary things conceivable. Depression is apt to turn us away from the ordinary common place things of God's creation, but whenever God comes, the inspiration to do the most natural simple things— the things we would never have imagined God was in, and as we do them we find He is there. The inspiration that comes to us in this way is an initiative against depression; we have to do the next thing and do it in the inspiration of God. If we

do a thing in order to overcome depression, we deepen the depression; but if the Spirit of God makes us feel intuitively that we must do the thing, and we do it, the depression is gone. Immediately we arise and obey, we enter on a higher plane of life.

Whatever you do, do it for God's glory. When we act like this, our life will become what it is suppose to. When we get frustrated with the mundane, we will not sense His hand on our life. When we wait on Him for inspiration and then act on that, we will overcome despair.

I love to read the older stuff that was written in the 1800s. It seems that, although they understood that the world was out there and all the vices and immorality were a real fact, it seems that there was more of a sense of God to them. They had fewer distractions, and it seems that many of the writers were tuned in, in a way that I don't see or feel today. I know that sometimes we can romanticize the past, and as much as I have read about the old time saints, they have had good points and bad. It seems though, that back then there was less distraction, let's face it there was less distraction. Jesus said that the word of God could be drowned out by the cares, worries and pleasures of this life (Mark 4:19).

There are legitimate pleasures and things to do and illegitimate pleasures. Paul said that all things were permissible but not all things were profitable (1 Cor. 6:12-14). God called us to live in the world but not be of the world. That means we can enjoy the legitimate things without guilt but we are aware that the time is short and things are passing away and we need to redeem the time (Eph. 5:15-16). Time is short. But to go on a vacation or watch a TV show is not necessarily sin unless you know for a fact that God has told you to do something else. No doubt we must be in tune to the Spirit, but sometimes we get so religious that we feel like if we are not praying, reading or witnessing we are out of God's will. This is not right. Things are not always cut and dried, but instead of becoming overwhelmed by the complexities we should embrace the simplicity of faith and, like a child, simply love God. A child lives and has fun. They do things that make them happy and are relatively unconcerned with life. They have faith that everything will be alright. They are not worried that they didn't tell their parents how great they were. When my sons were younger they would tell me that they loved me. They still do. I didn't tell them to tell me they just did. We tell God we love Him because we do. This has to come out of our heart as we come to know and experience Him as a son to a father.

My hope in this work is that many who have been crushed by what was supposed to help them would rethink the issues. Many who were told that they did not have enough faith and that was the reason for their problems or for not being healed, would recognize that this may not be so. If you have been drinking all your life and are suffering from liver issues, then your sin has indeed caused your disease (which God can heal and have mercy on you still), but if you have a disease that is no fault of your own, you have no reason to be condemned. You may legitimately go to the Lord and ask for healing. If no healing comes then realize that you may receive the ultimate healing in heaven and the answers that you are desperate for in this life will not really matter there.

If you're in the middle of a hard time, know that you're not alone. I have found that it is better to learn from someone else's pain and mistakes than your own. Also by hearing someone's struggle, it can help bring a clearer focus to our own struggles. We all struggle, the question is, are we dealing with our struggles and learning from them what we are supposed to? This life is brief; the Bible says it's a vapor (James 4:14). It has been said, "'Tis one life will soon be passed only what's done for Christ will last." What I am telling you are not just things I have read from a book, these are things that I have gone through, and I realize that if I don't learn something from them, and then try to help someone, it is in vain. That is the reason for this book.

Again, in America and in the modern churches so much is made of the outward. Money, position, fame. All these things have to do with the outward, and yet Paul said that the kingdom of God is not eating and drinking (not about the externals) but righteousness, peace and joy in the Holy Spirit (Rom. 10:17). To be made strong inwardly, many times things need to be taken so that other things may be added. L.B. Cowman talks about this in reference to Psalm 51:17:

"The sacrifices of God are a broken spirit; a
broken and contrite heart, O God you will
not despise." Those people God uses most

to bring glory to Himself are those who are completely broken, for the sacrifice He accepts is a "broken and contrite heart." It was not until Jacob's natural strength was broken, when "his hip was wrenched" at Peniel (Gen. 32:25), that he came to the point where God could clothe him with supernatural power. And it was not until Moses struck the rock at Horeb, breaking its surface, that cool "water came out of it for the people to drink (Ex. 17:6). It was not until Gideon's three hundred specially chosen soldiers "broke the jars that were in their hands" (Judg.7:19), which symbolizes brokenness in their lives, that the hidden light of the torch shone forth, bringing terror to their enemies. It was once the poor widow broke the seal on her only remaining jar of oil and began to pour it that God miraculously multiplied it to pay her debts and thereby supplied her means of support (2 Kings 4:1-7). It was not until Esther risked her life and broke through the strict laws of a heathen king's court that she obtained favor to rescue her people from death (Est. 4:16). It was once Jesus took the "five loaves... and broke them" (Luke 9:16) that the bread was multiplied to feed the five thousand. Through the very process of the loaves being broken, the miracle occurred.

Some will shiver at the thought of being broken, but as you read on, I want you to see that you being broken is only going to cause you to be better and stronger.
It was when Mary broke her beautiful "alabaster jar of very expensive perfume" (Matt. 26:7), destroying its future usefulness and value, that the wonderful fragrance filled the house. And it was when Jesus allowed His precious body to be broken by thorns, nails, and a spear that His inner life was poured out like an ocean of crystal-clear water for thirsty sinners to drink and live. It is not until the beautiful kernel of corn is buried and broken in the earth by death that its inner heart sprouts, producing hundreds of other seeds or kernels. And so it has always been that down through the history of plants, people and all of spiritual life-God uses broken things. Those who have been gripped by the power of the Holy Spirit and are used for God's glory are those who have been broken in their finances, broken in their self will, broken in their ambitions, broken in their lofty ideals, broken in their worldly reputation, broken in their desires, and often broken in their health. Yes, He uses those who are despised by the world and who seem totally hopeless and helpless, just as Isaiah said "The lame will carry off the plunder" (Is. 33:23).

Nobody wants to suffer. I do not want my kids or anyone else's kids to suffer, but the fact is very few will escape this life without a certain degree of suffering and the good news is that it does have value. I know I have already alluded to this, but many in the Charismatic and Pentecostal movements over the years have given the impression that you can avoid suffering if your faith is strong enough. And if you suffer, oh well, you must not have a strong faith. Suffering and pain are viewed as completely negative and of no value whatsoever. Judgments are made on people who suffer that are harsh and, in many cases, undeserved.

John wrote, "I pray that you prosper in all things and be in health, just as your soul prospers" (3 John 1:2). Again for those who take the Bible seriously, this can give the impression that, if you're not one hundred percent healthy and rich, then your soul must not be prospering. In contrast, if you are rich and well then that is proof that your soul is prospering. Under this thinking, the Hollywood crowd is totally blessed and the ones who are suffering financially or in poor health obviously are rejected by God. In God's economy it is just the opposite. This particular verse has reference to John's desire for the well being of the people, in the same way as if you were writing a friend, saying, "I hope all is well and that you continue to prosper and have a blessed life inside and out." This verse was never intended to be used as a measuring rod for someone's faith. Sad to say, though, it has.

Suffering, pain and all kinds of problems are apart of a fallen race; none of us will escape. Jesus said, "in the world you will have tribulation but be of good cheer I have overcome the world" (John 16:33). God does heal today and we should trust that this is true. As I said earlier, there are two sides to a coin and the other side of this coin is that sometimes He does not, even though we ask Him to. The Bible is full of the fact of God and His control of the world and His ultimate good plan for all of us. This plan carries on into eternity. Time is an interlude. Earth is a proving ground. Jim Elliot, missionary to the Aucas Indians in Ecuador, said, "He is no fool who gives up what he cannot keep to gain what he cannot lose."

Giving up my right to "know it all" is part of that giving up. Trying mentally to figure it all out will not bring the answers. I also realize that God does not expect us to know it all or understand it all. Trust in God and believe His word. This, and this only, will bring you peace and a deep sense of purpose and direction now and forever. No matter what comes into your life, no matter how great the pain, turn to God all the time and never give up.

It is written in Hebrews 11:6: "But without faith it is impossible to please Him, for he who comes to God must first believe that He is, and He is the rewarder of those who diligently seek Him." You may not have received the reward you think you need or deserve, but you can believe that He will bless you and that, no matter what happens, He will never leave you or forsake you (Heb. 13:5).

Sources

The author quotes liberally from the following, and recommends these works to the reader:

Chambers, Oswald, *My Utmost for His Highest*, Barbour Publishing, Inc., 1988 (original 1935).

Crabb, Larry, *Shattered Dreams: God's Unexpected Path to Joy*, WaterBrook Press, 2002.

Colson, Charles, with Fickett, Harold, *The Good Life*, Tyndale House Publishers, 2005.

Cowman, L.B., *Streams in the Desert*, Zondervan, 1999.

Friedman, Thomas, *The World is Flat: A Brief Guide to the Twenty-first Century*, Farrar, Straus and Giroux, 2005.

Hanegraaff, Hank, *Christianity in Crisis,* Harvest House Publishers, 1993.

Hunt, Dave, and McMahon, T.A., *The Seduction of Christianity: Spiritual Discernment in the Last Days*, Harvest House Publishers, 2005.

Martin, Walter, *Kingdom of the Cults,* Bethany House, 2003.

Piper, John, *Future Grace*, Multnomah, 2005.

Piper, John, *Desiring God* Inter-varsity Press, 2004.

Reeves, Christopher, *Nothing is Impossible: Reflections on a New Life*, Random House, 2002.

Wilkerson, David, *The Cross and the Switchblade*, Fleming H. Revel Company, 1965.